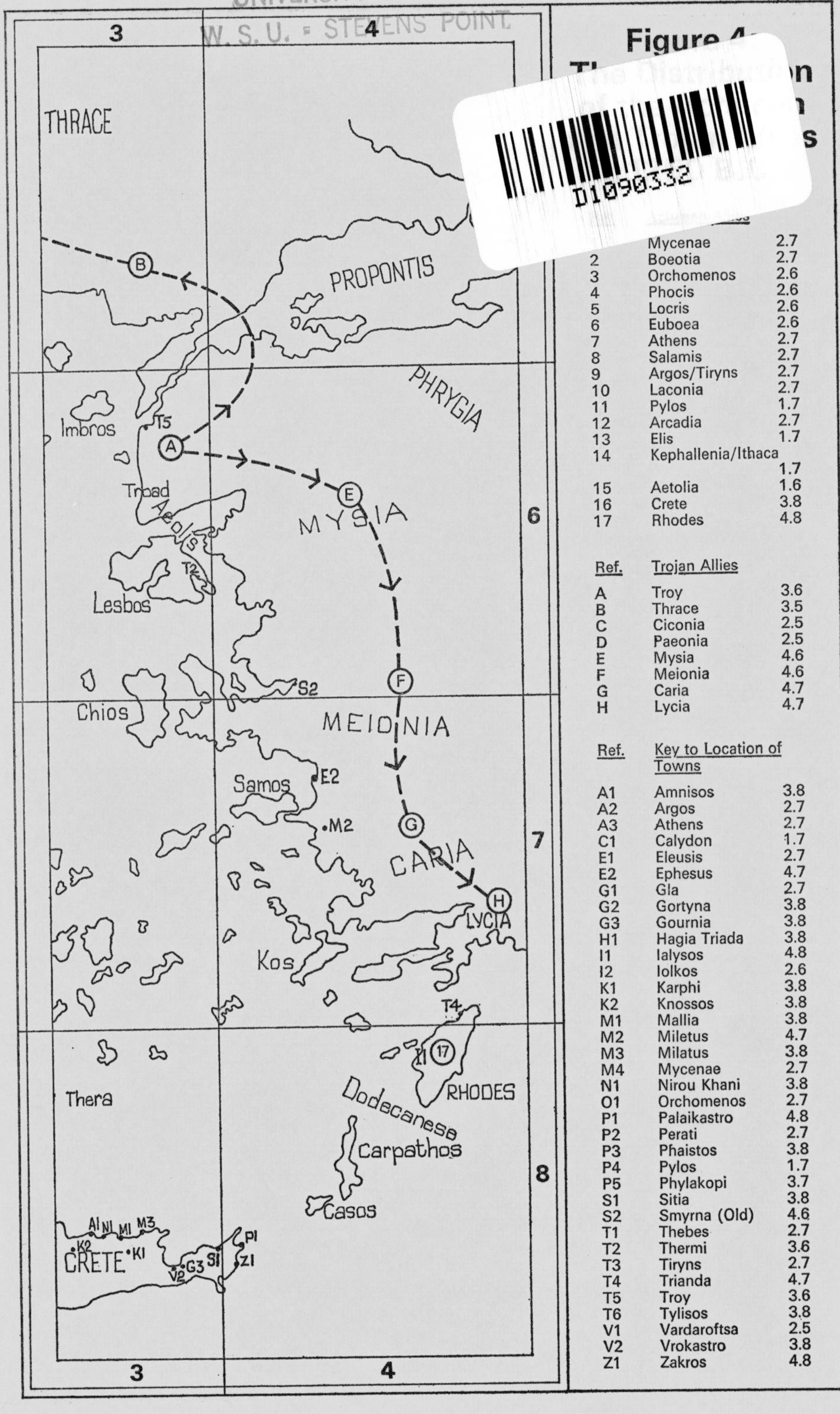
Figure 4:
3
4
THRACE
PROPONTIS
PHRYGIA
B
A
T5
Imbros
Troad
Aeolis
E
MYSIA
T2
Lesbos
S2
F
Chios
MEIONIA
Samos
E2
M2
G
CARIA
H
LYCIA
Kos
T4
I1
17
RHODES
Thera
Dodecanese
Carpathos
Casos
A1 N1 M1 M3
K2
CRETE K1
V2 G3 S1
P1
Z1
6
7
8
Mycenae 2.7
2 Boeotia 2.7
3 Orchomenos 2.6
4 Phocis 2.6
5 Locris 2.6
6 Euboea 2.6
7 Athens 2.7
8 Salamis 2.7
9 Argos/Tiryns 2.7
10 Laconia 2.7
11 Pylos 1.7
12 Arcadia 2.7
13 Elis 1.7
14 Kephallenia/Ithaca 1.7
15 Aetolia 1.6
16 Crete 3.8
17 Rhodes 4.8
Ref. Trojan Allies
A Troy 3.6
B Thrace 3.5
C Ciconia 2.5
D Paeonia 2.5
E Mysia 4.6
F Meionia 4.6
G Caria 4.7
H Lycia 4.7
Ref. Key to Location of Towns
A1 Amnisos 3.8
A2 Argos 2.7
A3 Athens 2.7
C1 Calydon 1.7
E1 Eleusis 2.7
E2 Ephesus 4.7
G1 Gla 2.7
G2 Gortyna 3.8
G3 Gournia 3.8
H1 Hagia Triada 3.8
I1 Ialysos 4.8
I2 Iolkos 2.6
K1 Karphi 3.8
K2 Knossos 3.8
M1 Mallia 3.8
M2 Miletus 4.7
M3 Milatus 3.8
M4 Mycenae 2.7
N1 Nirou Khani 3.8
O1 Orchomenos 2.7
P1 Palaikastro 4.8
P2 Perati 2.7
P3 Phaistos 3.8
P4 Pylos 1.7
P5 Phylakopi 3.7
S1 Sitia 3.8
S2 Smyrna (Old) 4.6
T1 Thebes 2.7
T2 Thermi 3.6
T3 Tiryns 2.7
T4 Trianda 4.7
T5 Troy 3.6
T6 Tylisos 3.8
V1 Vardaroftsa 2.5
V2 Vrokastro 3.8
Z1 Zakros 4.8

THE RISE OF THE DORIANS

THE RISE OF THE DORIANS

IVOR GRAY NIXON

FREDERICK A. PRAEGER, *Publishers*
New York · Washington

BOOKS THAT MATTER

Published in the United States of America in 1968
by Frederick A. Praeger, Inc., Publishers
111 Fourth Avenue, New York, N.Y. 10003

Library of Congress Catalog Card Number: 68-27092

Typography & Cover Design
by Mainwaring Muir

Printed in Great Britain

Contents

List of Illustrations

Figure

Acknowledgements

I SHOULD like to take this opportunity to thank the authors, translators, editors and publishers listed below for permission to quote from their works:

(1) The Harvard University Press, the Loeb Classical Library, for two passages from: *Arrian* (Introduction: references 3 and 5); and one passage from Demosthenes: *Third Philippic,* translated by Vince, J. H. (Introduction: reference 2).

(2) The Clarendon Press, Oxford, for:

a. Five passages from Hammond, N. G. L.: *A History of Greece to 322 B.C.* (Chapter 2: reference 30; Chapter 3: references 2 and 17; Chapter 4: reference 7; and Chapter 5: reference 7).

b. Two passages from Palmer, L. R. and Boardman, J.: *The Date of the Knossos Tablets* (Chapter 5: reference 30).

c. One passage from Desborough, V. R. d'A.: *The Last Mycenaeans and their Successors* (Chapter 4: reference 39).

(3) Associated Book Publishers Ltd., Methuen and Co. Ltd., London, for:

a. Five passages from Hall, H. R.: *The Ancient History of the Near East* (Chapter 2: references 16, 19, and 20; and Chapter 7: reference 13).

b. One passage from Pendlebury, J. D. S.: *The Archaeology of Crete* (Chapter 5: reference 31).

c. Together with St. Martin's Press Inc., New York, one passage from MacKendrick, P.: *The Greek Stones Speak* (Chapter 11: reference 8).

(4) Thomas Nelson and Sons Ltd. and the New American Library, for one passage from Homer's: *The Iliad,* translated by Rouse, W. H. D. (Chapter 7: reference 15).

(5) Penguin Books Ltd., for:

a. Eight passages from Hutchinson, R. W.: *Prehioricst Crete* (Chapter 5: references 1, 2, 4, 5 and 8; and Chapter 9: reference 49).

b. One passage from Seton Lloyd: *Early Anatolia* (Chapter 2: reference 22).
c. Four passages from Gurney, O. R.: *The Hittites* (Chapter 2: references 24 and 28; Chapter 3: reference 11; and Chapter 9: reference 39).
d. One passage from Woolley, L.: *A Forgotten Kingdom,* Pelican Books, 1953 (Chapter 9: reference 20).

(6) Archaeological Institute of America, *American Journal of Archaeology, 65,* for one passage from an article by Kohler, Ellen L. and Ralph, Elizabeth K. (Introduction: reference 1).

(7) Longmans Green and Co. Ltd., for one passage from Mellor, J. W.: *A Comprehensive Treatise on Inorganic and Theoretical Chemistry* (Chapter 9: reference 39).

(8) Faber and Faber, Ltd., London, and Alfred A. Knopf Inc., New York, for twelve passages from Palmer, Leonard R.: *Mycenaeans and Minoans* (Chapter 2: reference 1; Chapter 4: references 13, 16, 17 and 18; Chapter 5: references 17, 22, 23 and 25; Chapter 6: reference 1; and Chapter 8: reference 18).

(9) Max Parrish and Co., Limited, London, for one passage from Pendlebury, J. D. S.: *A Handbook to the Palace of Minos* (Chapter 4: reference 8).

(10) Pan Books, Ltd., London, for one passage from Seltman, Charles: *The Twelve Olympians* (Chapter 5: reference 35).

(11) Bantam Books Inc., New York, for three passages from Thucydides: *The Peloponnesian War,* translated by Benjamin Jowett, 1960 (Introduction: reference 6; Chapter 4: references 27 and 40).

(12) Times Newspapers Ltd., London, for a passage from an article in *The Times* by Palmer, L. R., and Gurney, O. R., *New Light Thrown on Ancient Crete,* 17th July 1964 (Chapter 5: reference 20).

(13) Professor G. E. Mylonas and the American School of Classical Studies, Athens, for two passages from *Priam's Troy and the Date of its Fall,* Hesperia, 33, 1964 (Chapter 8: reference 6).

I should also record my grateful thanks to the authors, editors, publishers and others, listed below, for permission to reproduce the illustrations and figures detailed, and for help given in making this possible:

(1) The Department of Antiquities, Ashmolean Museum and The Clarendon Press, Oxford, for two photographs from Boardman, J. and Palmer, L. R.: *The Date of the Knossos Tablets,* 1963 (Plates V and VI).

(2) The Clarendon Press, Oxford, for a Chronological Table from Hammond, N. G. L.: *A History of Greece to 322 B.C.,* 1959 (Figure 3).

(3) William Belknap, Jr., and the National Geographic Society for two photographs from: *The National Geographic,* February 1964 (Plate 1).

(4) Faber and Faber, Ltd., London, and Alfred A. Knopf Inc., New York, for a map from Palmer, L. R.: *Mycenaeans and Minoans* (Figure 5).

(5) Penguin Books, Ltd., for:

a. one illustration from Hutchinson, R. W.: *Prehistoric Crete,* 1962 (Figure 1).

b. one photograph from Seton Lloyd: *Early Anatolia,* 1956 (Plate VIII).

To Tina and Tony Wilson,
without whose help
and encouragement this book
would not have been possible

Introduction

Hail, Emperor, those about to die salute thee
SUETONIUS

THIS book deals with the Dorians whose origins are so remote in time that they are obscured by the distance of the past. Their emergence as a decisive force in Ancient Greece is so blurred by time that it is now possible to distinguish only a part of the pattern, and that part only with the greatest difficulty and lack of precision. Our cultural debt to Greece is directly traceable to the Athenian schools of thought, and for this reason the popular image of the Dorians is distorted. If we follow the relations between the Dorians and the Athenians back into history and beyond into legend, we find that these two peoples were traditional enemies, whose rivalries culminated in historical times in the Peloponnesian Wars. So it is understandable that the Athenians described the Dorians in highly unfavourable terms and at the best damned them with faint praise.

The popular image of the Dorians, which has prevailed for a century, shows them as a wild and savage people who flooded into Greece from the north, looting, burning and destroying the highly-developed Mycenaean culture in their advance. So they are held responsible for ushering in the Dark Ages in Greece, while the Athenians are venerated for holding out against them, and preserving the seeds of Greek civilization to flower again in the Golden Age of Pericles. The writings and opinions of the Athenian philosophers and historians of this renaissance were the base on which modern opinion has been founded. They need to be re-examined to see how much they are coloured by Athenian prejudice and hatred.

These savage hordes are usually depicted bursting into Macedonia and Thessaly from the north, destroying everything before them, overrunning the Peloponnese, coming by ship across the Gulf of

Corinth to the northern shores of the peninsula, from where they overran all the remaining Mycenaean kingdoms of the south except Athens. It is often conceded that the Dorians were a Greek-speaking people, and the date attributed to the invasion and destruction of the Mycenaean kingdoms is usually the late 12th century B.C.—about 1120. But if we examine this representation against the record revealed by modern archaeology, some important discrepancies are found. It soon becomes apparent that the Mycenaean kingdoms were overrun about 1200 B.C. and not eighty years later.

Kohler and Ralph[1] confirm by C-14 dating the archaeologists' date for the destruction of Pylos:

> ". . . the C-14 dates calculated with the 5800 half-life value place all samples close to or earlier than 1200 B.C., the date estimated by Blegen and Rawson for the destruction of the site."

The order of accuracy assigned to these dates averages about plus or minus sixty years so that a very good correlation is obtained.

There is an unbroken record of Mycenaean culture in Macedonia and Thessaly throughout this period, and there is no evidence of the destruction of Mycenaean centres there to indicate the arrival of barbaric invaders from the north until about 150 years *after* 1200 B.C. If a Mycenaean culture still prevailed in the invaded area, this hardly suggests that the conquests were made by barbaric hordes. Finally, the contemporary historical record, recently deciphered from the Linear B tablets, indicates that the invasion was expected from the south by sea and *not* overland from the north and west.

There are other discrepancies, and all lead to the conclusion that neither the facts nor the dates established agree with the traditional account of the Dorian invasion.

A critical re-examination of the available evidence has therefore been undertaken in this book, a survey leading to the conclusion that the traditional picture of the Dorian conquests of the Mycenaean kingdoms has to be revised. A number of theories to overcome the discrepancies have been evolved and are elaborated in some detail in the following chapters: the main theme is that the Dorians were Greeks, and that the decisive blow which destroyed the Mycenaean kingdoms was a sea-borne invasion of the Peloponnese from the coasts and islands of Asia Minor. The invasion was the last stage of a fratricidal struggle between north and south, between the northern Greeks and their allies and the more sophisticated southern Mycenaean kingdoms, whose origins pre-dated the Trojan War.

It was logical that the northerners, or Dorians, should attack their rivals at the weakest point of the Mycenaean empire: the recent conquests of the Trojan War scattered along the coasts of Asia Minor southwards from Troy; and that their initial success should lead on to the overrunning of the weakened Hittite empire and an amphibious drive southwards towards the Egyptian border. The repulse of this "push" made them naturally choose the normal sea-route home to Greece from the south-east corner of the Mediterranean: via the island chain which includes Rhodes and Crete. The returning armada attacked the original enemy at Pylos, the "soft underbelly" of the Mycenaean empire. Their success and consolidation led on to the undermining and collapse of the Mycenaean civilization.

The conclusions reached are unorthodox. For this I offer no apology, as progress demands the consideration of theories based on new evidence so that these can be tested against future investigations and discoveries. That the Dorians were Greek, and not just Greek-speaking, we know from Demosthenes,[2] who attacked Philip of Macedonia in these words:

> ". . . neither the Greek nor the barbarian world is big enough for the fellow's ambition. For that Philip, *like the recurrence* or attack *of a fever* or some other disease, is threatening even those who think themselves out of reach, of that not one of you is ignorant. Ay, and you know this also, that the wrongs which the Greeks suffered from the Lacedaemonians, or from us, *they suffered at all events at the hands of true-born sons of Greece,* and they might have been regarded as the acts of a legitimate son . . . who should be guilty of some fault or error in the management of his estate; . . . yet it could not be said that it was not one of the blood, not the lawful heir who was acting thus . . . Philip . . . is not only no Greek nor related to the Greeks, (he is) not even a barbarian from any place that can be named with honour, but a pestilent knave from Macedonia, whence it was never yet possible to buy a decent slave." (The italics are mine.)

Demosthenes lived closer to the time of the destruction of the Mycenaean empire and could repeat history handed down by oral tradition. To refer to the Dorians (or Lacedaemonians) as true Greeks was to identify them with the Mycenaeans. So it is no surprise to find that the artifacts and potsherds unearthed by the archaeologists in Macedonia and Thessaly, in strata corresponding to the period *before and after* the Dorian invasions about 1200 B.C., and in the Mycenaean kingdoms overrun by the Dorians, are in fact Mycenaean.

This does not imply that the Dorians were necessarily as sophisticated as their southern kinsmen. No doubt also they were hardier, more warlike, and less inclined to dwell in towns based on highly-organized palace hierarchies. We must see them rather as a pastoral people living in crofts and villages in much the same way as their Spartan descendants.

Demosthenes speaks of the *recurrence of a fever,* a parallel which becomes clearer if we consider the course followed by Philip's son, Alexander the Great, from Macedonia down to Egypt, an invasion route almost identical with the one the Dorians and allies would have chosen to overrun the Hittite empire and push southwards towards the Egyptian border. Alexander studied in the Greek schools at Athens, and was intensely interested in the Homeric legends of Troy, so we can guess that some tradition of this route may have lingered, and guided Alexander in choosing his invasion path.

To have achieved so much, the Dorians must have possessed a greater degree of power and organization than is generally admitted. About 1200 B.C. adequate sea-power must also have existed in the eastern Mediterranean for such a sea-borne invasion to be staged. Archaeological evidence is accumulating to show that at this time Macedonia and Thessaly were extensively settled by a people of Mycenaean culture, though less sophisticated than in the south. These people, and their north-eastern allies, were the most likely destroyers of the Hittite empire, since there is no evidence to show that the homelands of the Dorians and their allies were themselves overrun.

A people strong enough to bring down the Hittite empire would certainly have been capable of a sea-borne invasion of southern Greece; and we have the written evidence of the Egyptian inscriptions and murals that the invaders who reached the Egyptian border had a powerful fleet. The maritime centres of the eastern Mediterranean—Troy, Rhodes, Cyprus, Byblos, Sidon and others—were all in their hands together, no doubt, with most of the fleets based upon them.

Nearly 900 years later Alexander the Great, in his speech at Tyre,[3] talked of a similar naval strategy:

> "Nor is it safe to pursue Darius, leaving in our rear the city of Tyre . . . But with Tyre once destroyed, Phoenicia could all be held, and the best and strongest part of the Persian navy, the Phoenician element, *would most probably come over to us*. For neither the rowers nor the mariners of Phoenicia will have the courage, if their cities are in our hands, to sail the sea and run its dangers for the sake of others . . ." (The italics are mine.)

Alexander's prophecy, made while the Persians still held control of the sea, was correct: once the coastal forts had fallen to his land-based armies the fleets which operated from them joined forces with the Greeks and gained control of the sea.

Such fleets would have been sufficient for the Dorians, too, and more evidence is coming to light that sea-trade in Mycenaean times was more extensive and better organized than had been realized, and that such trading had already been flourishing then for about a thousand years.[4]

The success of the invasion of Pylos from the sea would have been followed by incursions direct from the Dorian homeland of the north into the Mycenaean kingdoms. If it seems unlikely that the Dorians could have shown such a high degree of organization, the example of Alexander of Macedonia, nearly 900 years later, indicates how effectively a pastoral people could be organized:[5]

> ". . . For Philip found you vagabonds and helpless, most of you clothed with sheepskins, pasturing a few sheep on the mountain-sides and fighting for these, with ill success . . . Philip gave you cloaks to wear . . . brought you down from the hills to the plains, made you doughty opponents of your neighbouring enemies . . . He made you dwellers of cities; and civilized you . . . opened up commerce to your country; and enabled you to work your mines in peace. Then he made you overlords of the Thracians, before

whom you had long died of terror, and, humbling the Phocians, made the highway into Greece broad and easy for you . . . All these noble deeds of my father towards you are great indeed, if looked at by themselves, and yet small if compared with ours . . . I set forth from that country which hardly maintained you in comfort, and at once opened to you the strait of the Hellespont, though the Persians were then masters of the sea . . . All good things from Egypt and Cyrene, which I took without striking a blow, come to you; the Syrian valley and Palestine and Mesopotamia are your possessions; . . . the wealth of Lydia; the treasures of Persia; the good things of India, the outer ocean, all are yours . . ."

We still have to find an explanation for the Dark Ages, for the widespread depopulation and the disruption of Mycenaean civilization. This is probably to be found not in the wars themselves but rather in a devastating plague or plagues. Thucydides[6] records a saying current long before his time:

"A Dorian War will come and a plague with it", and remarks that: "men's memories reflected their sufferings."

Perhaps it is significant that after this period of suffering the Gorgon's Head became a familiar motif in Greek art, epitomizing all the superstitious terror of such an event. For this reason I have chosen the Gorgon's Head used to decorate the handles of the great bronze krater found in the treasure of Vix, for the jacket of this book. This magnificent work of art symbolizes not only the terrors of the Dark Ages, but also shows a high level of technical achievement which could hardly have evolved in a few decades, but must undoubtedly have owed much to the metallurgical achievements of the Minoan and Mycenaean bronzeworkers and to the Hittite metallurgists who preceded them.

It was from this period of suffering and chaos that the Greek renaissance rose, refined and purified of the less noble features of the Mycenaean and Minoan cultures. Without the sufferings of the Dark Ages it is doubtful if the Golden Age of the Greek renaissance could have reached the heights it did achieve, and for this we owe on balance some debt of gratitude to the Dorians.

It is appropriate that I should acknowledge my debt to all the authorities listed in the bibliography appearing at the end of each chapter for the data and quotations which I have derived from them. In particular I should like to mention C. W. Blegen, V. R. d'A. Desborough, O. R. Gurney, N. G. L. Hammond, R. W. Hutchinson and L. R. Palmer, not only for the noteworthy contributions they have made in this field of study but also for the great pleasure I have derived from reading their works.

I. G. Nixon, Matterhorngniss, Zermatt, Switzerland, 1967

REFERENCES

[1] Kohler, Ellen L. and Ralph, Elizabeth K., American Journal of Archaeology, 65, p. 367.

[2] Demosthenes, *Third Philippic,* translated by J. H. Vince, pp. 31–5.

[3] Arrian, The Loeb Classical Library, Harvard University Press, II, 17, 1–4.

[4] Sibylle von Cleo-Reden, *The Realm of the Great Goddess,* 1961, pp. 58–64 and 100–101.

[5] Arrian, *ibid,* VII, 9, 1–9.

[6] Thucydides, *The Peloponnesian War*, Bantam Classic, 1960, Book II, p. 124f.

CHAPTER ONE

Uncovering the Past

Let no man enter who knows no geometry

PLATO

THE period during which the Mycenaean empire flourished and fell is one of abiding interest to anyone who has read Homer with enjoyment. The period of its fall, about the beginning of the twelfth century B.C., witnessed a number of other stirring events: the fall of the Hittite empire and the invasion of Egypt by "The Peoples of the Sea", together with other incidents closely related to them. It is the purpose of this work to investigate the part played by the Dorians in this crucial period, and their influence on that great development of Greek thought in the Classical Age which laid some of the more important foundation-stones of our modern culture.

The Greeks of the classical period traced their origin back to their ancestors of the Heroic Age who had fought and intrigued at Troy. We in our turn find the source of our modern way of life, and the origin of democracy, in the developments of the arts, philosophy and science which took place in Ancient Greece in the period following the Dark Ages. Therefore the course of events at this time is of the greatest interest to us all, as it was then that the evolution of our present civilization first gathered momentum.

However, all this happened three thousand years or so ago, so that the traces have to a great extent been lost in the mists of antiquity. In recent years archaeologists have unearthed inscriptions and written records dating back to that time, and these have given us a few basic historical facts which can act as a sure foundation for reconstructing the pattern of events. The preservation of these historical records to this day is the fortuitous outcome of the artistic and technological developments which took place in those ancient times.

We are fortunate in having these few written records for our guidance. They have come down to us because, in the artistic field, the Egyptians used frescoes and wall-paintings for the commemoration of important events, or for the glorification of the dead on the walls of their tombs. Also they often annotated these pictorial records with a written inscription giving the details of the story. Also, in the technological field, man had long ago learnt the use of clay for making vessels for cooking and storage and had developed the process for firing the green clay to produce a hard and weatherproof utensil. With the invention of writing this vehicle was used at a very early stage as the plastic medium for recording the written words, and for their preservation as a permanent record by baking the tablet after making the impression on its surface. Where permanent records were not needed it was also customary to sun-dry the green clay after the record had been made, and these sun-dried tablets proved adequate for such a purpose.

Originally the use of writing, and its recording on clay tablets, seems to have been devoted to recording storehouse inventories and for other purposes of trade. At the same time the larger Temple States began to use this tool for recording treaties, diplomatic correspondence and for maintaining foreign office and historical records. The Egyptians and Hittites were amongst those who used such records. For our purpose in considering the rise and fall of the Mycenaean empire, the Egyptian and Hittite records, together with others of this type, are of the greatest value, since they record the events of the time and their contacts with the Mycenaeans and their contemporaries.

With the Mycenaeans themselves we are less fortunate as the contemporary written records surviving are mainly storehouse inventories and trade records, most of which were made on sun-dried tablets. It is fortunate for the preservation of these temporary records that major disasters, such as the capture and sack of a city, often resulted in the place being burnt to the ground, so that the sun-dried tablets were fortuitously baked in the resulting holocaust to give a permanent record. Only a few tablets known from Greece or Crete at that time are believed to have been baked specifically to preserve them permanently, together with a few inscribed stone or clay votive offerings, and a number of amphorae marked with certain trade data such as the place of origin.

The Cretan and Mycenaean archives which we have been able to translate with certainty are all written in a type of script known as a "syllabary", in which the signs stand for combinations of vowels with consonants. The key to this was found by a young architect called Michael Ventris. Ventris was able to demonstrate that this writing—which was christened Linear B script—was in fact an early form of Greek virtually identical with the Achaean (or Arcado-Cyprian) dialect which survived in Cyprus and Arcadia into historical times. This Linear B script, which in Mycenaean times (principally 1400–1200 B.C.) prevailed in both Greece and Crete, had been preceded in Crete by an earlier script known as Linear A, which was also a "syllabary" but not Greek. The latter, in turn, was preceded by a still earlier Minoan script written in hieroglyphics, or picture signs, which owed something to the Egyptians. This last script has not yet been interpreted. The Linear A script apparently shows affinities with languages spoken on the mainland of the eastern Mediterranean: with Luvian, according to Palmer's researches; and with a Western Semitic language, according to those of Cyrus H. Gordon. These experts are under the severe handicap of having to work with very limited material, as the number of records in Linear A script so far unearthed is relatively few. Further finds will throw more light on this language, which possibly may be a Minoan *lingua franca* used for bureaucratic records and trade purposes.

The full account of the decipherment and interpretation of the Linear B script is a separate story which has been dealt with by Palmer and Chadwick in vivid and convincing terms.[1] These records, therefore, are written history, which together with the Egyptian, Hittite and other records give us a contemporary account which we must accept as the basis of our reconstruction of events at that time. Of course, as in the case of all written history, we have to bear in mind the tendency to distort the picture for nationalistic reasons, and the fact that the interpretations and identifications of the places and peoples involved cannot always be made with absolute certainty. Subject to these qualifications, which must be kept in mind throughout the subsequent discussions, we have no right to ignore the written record which we must take as our basis and which the pattern of events deduced must fit.

Naturally, after the lapse of three thousand years or more, the number of recorded historical facts which have come down from this period in the Egyptian, Hittite, Minoan, Mycenaean, Ugarit and other tablets and inscriptions is very few. They are mainly limited to the Egyptian and Hittite records, but taken together they still add up to an important body of factual information. It is unfortunate that the Mycenaean and Minoan data are mainly limited to storehouse and administrative records, and that with the fall of Knossos, Pylos and the other royal palaces in Crete and on the Greek mainland, the keeping of these bureaucratic records apparently ceased. At least, if they continued, no discoveries of later archives have yet been made. Indeed, it has often been claimed that, with the end of the Minoan and Mycenaean civilizations, the art of writing was lost during the Dark Ages in the Grecian world. I do not believe that this was the case, as in more recent times human experience has shown that the art of writing, and even literature, survived in those parts of the Roman empire which were completely overrun by incursive barbarians. Man is a thinking animal; once introduced to writing and literature the human mind is enthralled by them and does not lightly discard them. Therefore I do not think writing became a lost art, but survived in a limited form and indeed received an impetus in a new direction.

The use of clay tablets for compiling Linear B storehouse and administrative records was a traditional bureaucratic system, in which doubtless the clay tablet was hallowed by custom much in the same way as the English civil service clung to the quill pen and copperplate script long after they were outmoded. Moreover, clay tablets had for this purpose the advantage of preserving a relatively permanent record. We have, however, conclusive evidence that ink was used by Mycenaeans and Minoans, as clay cups have been discovered on which ink inscriptions had been recorded. It is also evident that more perishable materials than clay were used as writing material, since in Crete clay sealings, attributed to the period after the fall of the Palace of Knossos, have been found with traces of vegetable matter on the clay surface, indicating that the seals had been attached to more perishable documents.

There is strong presumptive evidence that such a sealing was attached to a document, since it was common practice for important people to use personal seals for the identification of property, and no doubt too as a signature. The art of engraving these seals was highly developed in Minoan areas, and was adopted by the Mycenaeans, doubtless as a result of their Cretan contacts. Many of these seals were beautifully executed in ivory, steatite or other stone, and were magnificent works of art in miniature (see Figure 1). Greek tradition also records that "skins" were used as writing material.

Figure 1. Minoan Sealing—Mother Goddess in High Place

This deduction that the art of writing still survived in the Aegean during the Dark Ages, in the period following the disasters of the twelfth century B.C., receives strong confirmation from a parallel example from Cyprus, which was in contact with the Aegean. Here a modified form of Minoan Linear Script, adopted in Cyprus *c* 1500 B.C., was still in use there during the period *c* 700–200 B.C.[2] No example has survived for the period 1050–700 B.C., *presumably because perishable materials were used.* What is true for Cyprus is equally true for Greece and Crete. It was not the art of writing that was lost but rather the practice of keeping bureaucratic records on clay tablets. This was discontinued because the traditional Palace systems which used it were destroyed by the changes and disasters following the Dorian incursions. Writing in the Aegean was directed from this time on towards the establishment of literature rather than factual records, but by the time the historical period was reached the written language—contrary to Cypriot example—had changed from a "syllabary" to writing based on an alphabet. The art of writing was not lost but merely changed.

In addition to written historical records which have survived, we have a valuable tool in the application of archaeological discoveries, which are in fact fossilized history, to help us reconstruct the pattern of events. Once the archaeologist has discovered the site of an ancient city the work of uncovering and interpreting the remains is a laborious and painstaking process which often takes years to complete. The deposits constituting the ancient site, usually in the form of a mound, may well be 40 to 50 feet thick or more. The mound can be compared with a gigantic layer-cake in which the archaeological layers, or strata, are piled one upon the other. Each stratum, as defined by the archaeologist, represents the life period of one phase of the settlement, brought to an end by a disaster such as earthquake, fire or sack, by the expiry of the natural life of the structures comprising the settlement, or sometimes by a change or modification in the culture of the people inhabiting the site. The detritus of living is preserved within each stratum: the artifacts left by the inhabitants of that phase of the settlement. A famous example of such a mound is the site of Hissarlik, or ancient Troy, admirably described by Blegen. Its fate, as we shall see below, was closely connected with that of the Mycenaean empire.

The archaeologist is often able to use these artifacts, such as pottery sherds, seals, jewellery, buttons and household articles, to date the strata in which they are found. It is customary to number each stratum in turn, starting usually with 1 as the oldest or bottom layer and numbering successively upwards (see Figure 2), and the period represented by each stratum is normally referred to by this number; for instance, the oldest settlement stratum in Troy is known as "Troy I". Main strata are often sub-divided into sub-strata, usually numbered Ia, Ib, Ic. Thus the settlement believed to be ancient Troy, whose siege was immortalized in the *Iliad*, is known as "Troy VIIa".

The artifacts are normally dated by cross-reference to similar ones found in other sites whose dates have already been established by

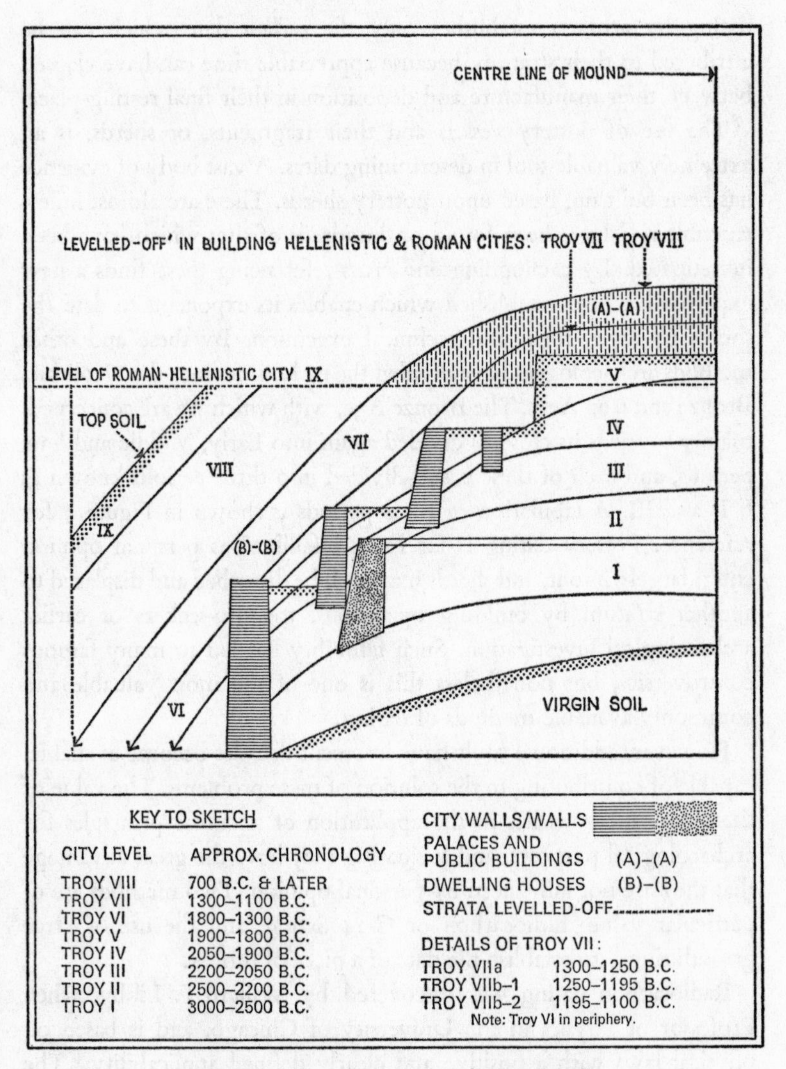

Figure 2. Troy: Cross-section of City Mound

historical records or other means. For instance, Egyptian scarabs and inscribed vessels can be dated by the reign of the king concerned which is known from the historical records. Natural phenomena such as celestial events recorded by astronomers, or earthquakes can often be dated from contemporary records. This method can be precise, but dating by artifacts establishes only the *earliest* date which can be attributed to their stratum, because appreciable time can have elapsed between their manufacture and deposition in their final resting-place.

The use of pottery vessels and their fragments, or sherds, is an extremely valuable tool in determining dates. A vast body of evidence has been built up, based upon pottery sherds. These are almost indestructible and have been found on hundreds of sites which have been investigated. By cataloguing and cross-referencing these finds a new expertise has been established which enables its exponents to date the sherds by style, form and technical execution. By these and other methods archaeologists have divided the early times into the Neolithic, Bronze and Iron Ages. The Bronze Age, with which we are concerned, mainly towards its close, is divided again into Early, Middle and Late periods, and each of these is sub-divided into three periods known as I, II and III. A tabulation of these periods is shown in Figure 3 for reference. Pottery dating is far from infallible[3] as personal opinion enters largely into it, and sherds may well be disturbed and displaced to another stratum by building operations, treasure-seekers or earlier archaeological investigation. Such fallibility has led to many famous controversies, but nonetheless this is one of the most valuable and commonly available methods of dating.

However, additional tools have in recent decades become available, capable of contributing to the solution of these problems. The value of these new methods lies in the application of scientific principles for archaeological purposes, and for dating they have the great advantage that they are not influenced by personal opinion. Two methods are of particular value: radiocarbon or C-14 dating, and the use of "tree growth rings" to establish the date of a piece of timber.

Radiocarbon dating was discovered by Willard F. Libby, when Professor of Physics in the University of Chicago, and is based on physical laws with a positive and clearly defined applicability.[4] The biosphere contains a certain amount of a radioactive form of carbon (C-14) produced from it by the action of cosmic rays. This isotope of carbon is "taken up" by any living carbonaceous matter, at the time it is formed, as a result of that part of the carbon cycle involved in the formation of living matter. Radiocarbon decays or disappears at a fixed rate from its moment of formation; so after 5730 years, the

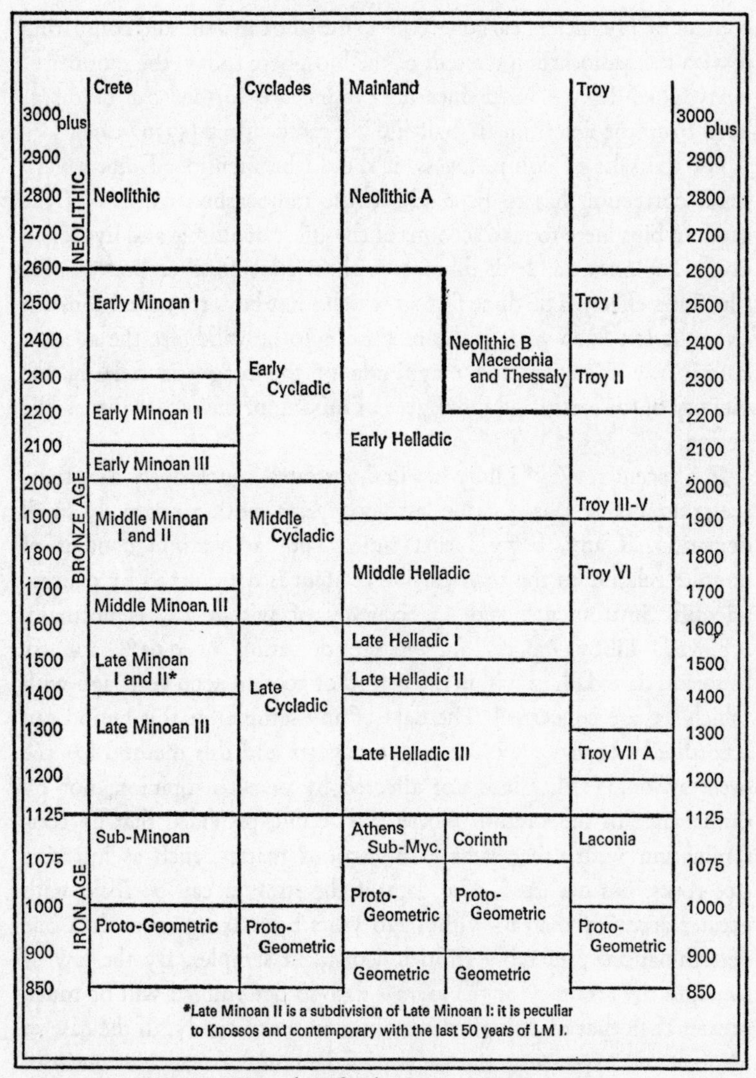

Figure 3. Time-chart for the Aegean, c 3000–850 B.C.

"half-life" of radiocarbon, one half of the radiocarbon present at the moment of formation will have gone. Provided that three factors have remained constant over the last 8000 years (the period over which radiocarbon dating can most usefully be applied), the method is a positive dating tool. By determining the present-day radiocarbon content of any ancient carbonaceous material from a site and comparing it with the radiocarbon content of the biosphere today, the number of years which have elapsed since the sample was formed can be calculated from the determined "half-life" of radiocarbon (5730 years).

For the sake of completeness, it should be mentioned that a very small correction has to be made to the radiocarbon content of the modern biosphere to take account of the effect of atomic and hydrogen bomb explosions and for dilution with inactive fossil carbon dioxide (the Suess effect). The three factors which must have remained constant over the last 8000 years if the method is to be valid, are the average cosmic ray intensity, the magnitude of the magnetic field in the vicinity of the earth, and the degree of mixing of the oceans during the period.

In a recent review[4] Libby has demonstrated conclusively that these are constants, at least for the last 4000 years, with a relatively small deviation, if any, beyond that time. The radiocarbon content of samples relative to the total carbon content is determined by delicate scientific instruments, and an accuracy of within 2% is normally achieved—Libby reports an average deviation of 0.65% for six historical dates falling within the period of 3000 to 4000 years ago with which we are concerned. The date of any sample for this period can accordingly be fixed within, say, 120 years and this method has the great advantage that it is not affected by personal opinion, nor by disturbance of the stratum where it is found, provided that no contamination with other later carbonaceous matter, such as intrusive tree-roots, has occurred. The date of the stratum can be fixed with greater accuracy than to within 120 years by making more than one determination, preferably from independent samples. By the law of averages the accuracy of the *average* date so determined will be much greater than that of a single determination. Fortunately, in the case of Minoan and Mycenaean sites, many of the samples available consist of carbonized wood, cereals or beans which were preserved by the event which destroyed the site. Around 1200 B.C. many of these sites were sacked and burnt by the Dorians. Therefore plenty of samples are *potentially* available for dating by this method.

It is therefore to be hoped that this method will be applied extensively by archaeologists working in the Mycenaean and Minoan field.

The method is based on sound scientific principles, and the results could be of the greatest value if the tests are properly carried out on a *series* of samples whose archaeological origin is known. The fact that samples can be contaminated by intrusive roots, or "humic" contaminant, is a relatively minor factor in the problem, as the former can be detected when sampling and the latter can be removed in general by a simple chemical treatment. Certainly this factor in C-14 dating is a far less serious one than the ubiquitous "intrusive" sherds which so often bedevil the dating of strata by means of the interpretation of pottery styles.

One feature of this method must be kept clearly in mind: the C-14 date found for a sample applies to the date at which the organic material from which the sample was taken was first formed. Thus, for example, the date found for a sample of charcoal taken from a charred beam found in a destruction stratum applies not to the date at which the destruction took place, nor to that at which the structure was built in which the beam was incorporated, but to the date at which the wood (in the portion of the beam from which the sample was taken) was grown. The part of the beam from which the sample was taken, and whether the beam has been "squared" or re-used, is therefore of the greatest importance. Within a single large beam the date of the growth rings of wood can easily extend over a span of one hundred years, or more. For this reason the sample is best taken from the outer growth rings corresponding to the date at which the tree was felled. On the other hand samples of textiles, carbonized beans, cereals, olives and other crops are to be preferred for more precise dating as they correspond to the year when the crop was harvested, and therefore normally to the date at which the destruction took place.

A further scientific tool of potential value is tree ring dating or dendronology.[5] This is based on the fact that normally only one tree ring is formed each year and that—depending on the season—tree rings formed in any particular year vary in width. In a good growing season the width is greater than in a poor one. Thus the relative width of tree rings over a sequence of years forms a unique pattern; accordingly, by taking a cross-section from a piece of timber it is possible to calculate the period when that tree was growing. This is strikingly demonstrated by a typical sample from timber used *c* A.D. 1257 for building a Long House for Indians living in the Wetherill Mesa in Colorado (Plate 1). Fortunately the method can be applied equally well to carbonized specimens of wood. It is somewhat less accurate for establishing absolute dates than radiocarbon dating, as for the period 3000 to 3600 years ago an average deviation of 3% from the historical date can be expected.[6] This is probably connected with the fact that on very rare occasions more than one tree ring can be formed in one year. But the method should be potentially of great value for the *relative* dating of Mycenaean and Minoan sites as by comparing the tree ring patterns of carbonized timber from different sites, or from building done at different periods on the same site, it should be possible to establish relative datings with some accuracy if suitable samples are still available.

Unfortunately, although radiocarbon dating was invented in the years immediately after World War II, and tree ring dating just before it, neither method appears to have been applied by archaeologists on Minoan and Mycenaean sites. Virtually nothing has been published in this field, so that we cannot yet utilize either of these tools of precision for our task. The Greeks themselves, with their interest in new ideas, would surely not have neglected the problem so. It is to be hoped that all such scientific methods will soon be applied. Perhaps we should follow Plato's example and inscribe over the portals of our Schools of Archaeology the words: "Let no man enter who knows no geometry".

There remain two further tools which can be used: Greek tradition, and Human Behaviourism—that is, the tendency for mankind to react in a similar fashion under similar conditions, and for history to repeat itself. Neither of these is as strong or precise as history or archaeology, but they should not be neglected. Hammond has rightly emphasized that the oral tradition, which has come down in part through the literary works of the early classical writers, particularly Homer, Herodotus, Thucydides and Hesiod, may well contain an element of fact. I propose to make use of these traditions and myths where appropriate. Such use does not, of course, imply that these traditions can be followed blindly, or accepted always as immutable fact. The Greeks themselves—Thucydides and Herodotus in particular—clearly recognized that the old traditions were not always reliable. Thucydides[7] warned that the accounts of poets and chroniclers should not be taken too literally. Herodotus expressed scepticism about tales of heroes and gods which did not touch the core of Greek religious belief, and commented on one occasion: "The Greeks in general have a weakness for inventing stories with no basis of fact." The element of historical fact has to be separated from the heroic and divine myths in which it is embedded, and compared carefully with the available historical and archaeological data.

The use of historical parallels and the deduction of human reactions to a given situation based on past experience needs no elaboration, as it is a common and useful, though sometimes misused, tool.

In constructing a synthesis of historical and archaeological fact, Greek traditions and historical parallels, I will consider first the limited written record available (Chapter 2) and then set out seven basic theories (Chapter 3) which can be deduced from these records and other data. An examination of the historical background follows to bring out in more detail the way in which the theories were built up.

These theories cannot be applied dogmatically. More and more information is becoming available as new finds are made and new methods of investigation developed. It is to be hoped that the application of the more recent scientific methods described will contribute to our knowledge and increase the tempo with which it becomes available. The theories outlined in Chapter 3 will all be tested by this new information in due course, and by the more intensive review of already available information by experts in their own fields. Fresh discoveries will show to what extent the outline of these theories must be modified.

REFERENCES

[1] Palmer, L. R., *Mycenaeans and Minoans,* 1961; Chadwick, J., *The Decipherment of Linear B,* 1958.

[2] Hammond, N. G. L., *A History of Greece to 322 B.C.,* 1959, p. 93.

[3] Albright, W. F., *The Archaeology of Palestine,* Pelican Books, 1960, pp. 29f, 36, 38f.

[4] Libby, W. F., Antiquity, September 1963, p. 213f.

[5] Belknap, W., Jr., National Geographic, February 1964, p. 173f.

[6] Libby, W. F., Antiquity, September 1963, p. 217.

[7] Thucydides, *The Peloponnesian War,* Bantam Classic, 1960, Book I, p. 33.

CHAPTER TWO

The Historical Record and General Background

But where are the snows of yesteryear?

VILLON

IN recent years a number of historical facts have emerged regarding events in the Aegean/Middle East areas *c* 1200 B.C. Taken together, these help to throw some light on those events which led to the Dorian invasion and the subsequent Dark Ages. First of all we have the reported facts recorded in the state archives of the Hittite, Egyptian and Assyrian empires and the kingdom of Pylos. These records are contemporary written history and must be accepted as such with just as much force as, for instance, the records of the Middle Ages. Of course, like all written history, proper allowance must be made for exaggeration, chauvinism and political propaganda, while in some cases in addition an element of doubt exists regarding the interpretation of the names of people, tribes or nations mentioned in the records.

Subject to these limitations the records are factual and, as the sole written records of the period that we have, should be used as the basis of any attempt to deduce the course of events. In this connection an objective approach to these problems has undoubtedly suffered from the dead hand of authoritative opinion. For centuries the Homeric epics and the questions of the Grecian heritage to the civilized world have fascinated scholars, and more recently archaeologists, and have attracted many men of genius such as Evans. These men had to work without much of the benefit of the decipherment of the royal archives, which is now available, but by sheer genius, inspired interpretation of the archaeological record and Greek tradition, and by expertise in the interpretation of artistic form and technique in ceramics and other artifacts, they laid a firm foundation for the study and evaluation of these ancient civilizations. However, it is of great importance that the pioneer work done by these great men should not be accepted today as the final word in an evolving situation. It is essential that recent discoveries in the historical, archaeological and other fields should be utilized on their own merits in an endeavour to solve these problems, and that they should be interpreted when necessary without reference to preconceived views reached before this new information was available.

It is, therefore, of the greatest importance to review the new historical evidence now available to us in order to see whether any new theories can be postulated which may offer a better, or more complete explanation of those events which led up to and followed the Dorian invasion. Studies of the texts of the royal archives, which have been translated in recent years, reveal a few scattered but important facts. In order to deal with this matter scientifically it is proposed in each case first to consider the fact itself, and then the interpretations which have been placed on the text in question. Finally these interpretations will be further developed, where appropriate, against the main themes with which we are concerned.

1 The Invasion of Pylos

The decipherment of the Linear B tablets from Pylos has revealed that the invasion of the Pylian land was expected from the sea. These records have been vividly described and interpreted by Palmer[1] who refers to the vital tablet in the following words: "All important was the first tablet with its introductory explanatory sentence: 'How the watchers are guarding the coastal regions'." From Palmer's analysis[2] of the lists given in other tablets of women and children, and their rations, we gather that they were concentrated at two main points—Pylos in the "Hither" or Western Province and Leuktron in the "Further" Province. This distribution of refugees is again consistent with the anticipation of a sea-borne invasion. The whole Pylian archive is permeated by a sense of emergency, and other factors pointing in this direction can be cited: the movement of a ship's complement of thirty rowers to a place called Pleuron is recorded;[3] the transfer of masons "going to build" to the main centres of Pylos and Leuktron, where the refugees had been concentrated, presumably to repair the fortifications;[4] the allocation of "Temple bronze (as) points for spears and arrows";[5] even the issue of an emergency "iron ration" of pounded linseed[6] to the men recorded as coastal watchers is implied by one set of tablets. Possibly this linseed was mixed with poppyseed and honey by analogy with Thucydides' report[7] of the Spartans trapped on Sphacteria. Finally Palmer concludes his account of the archives of Pylos with the description of a set of tablets listing a series of household effects[8] which he believes to be an inventory of the contents of a Mycenaean royal tomb.

Authoritative opinion based on archaeological evidence assigns the date of the destruction of the Palace of Nestor, king of Pylos at the time of the siege of Troy, to *c* 1200 B.C.,[9] and equates it with the Dorian invasion and the destruction of other centres of power on the Greek mainland—including Mycenae and Tiryns—which occurred around the same period. The distribution of forces outlined in the tablets clearly indicates that the attack was anticipated from the sea, and not overland from the north across the Gulf of Corinth which was the traditional invasion route.[10] This view is further supported by the concentration of the women and children at the two main defence centres of Pylos and Leuktron on the sea-coast, which is consistent with the anticipation of a sea-borne invasion landing at some point unknown along the extensive sea-coast of the Pylian territory. Finally, it must be conceded that Palmer[11] produces strong arguments to show that the tablets listing a series of household effects are indeed the inventory of a Mycenaean tomb dedicated "when the Wanax buried Sja-ke-wa, son of Damocles". Palmer further identifies Sja-ke-wa, son of Damocles, from texts given in other tablets, as the Governor of the "Hither" Province and comments on the significance of the king himself officiating at the funeral. It is tempting to speculate that possibly this high official was killed in a preliminary brush with the Dorians and we will return to this aspect later (Chapter 4) when dealing with the fall of Pylos in more detail.

2 "*The Peoples of the Sea*"

The ancient Egyptian records refer to "The Peoples of the Sea" on a number of occasions. For our purpose the most significant records are:

(A) those which make it clear that the Trojans sided with the

Hittite empire during the thirteenth century wars against Egypt. The Egyptian scribes include the Dardanians, immortalized by Homer in the *Iliad,* amongst the Hittite allies mustered against the forces of Ramesses II and presumably present at the battle of Kadesh (*c* 1285 B.C.), as well as the Philistines and Sherden who were probably allies of the Trojans.[12]

(B) the records dealing with the attack on Egypt *c* 1221 B.C. by the Libyans together with a confederation of sea-raiders which included the Akaiwasha (or Achaeans) amongst the list of the more important nations or tribes involved.[13] This list includes moreover the Tursha, Luka and Shardana, who have been identified respectively with the Tursenoi, Lycians, and Sardinoi.

(C) the records dealing with a large scale attack *c* 1192 B.C. by land and sea on the eastern Marches of Egypt,[14] again by a confederation which included the Denyen (or Danaoi) in the list of the more important groups involved. This particular list mentions in addition the Peleset (or Philistines), Thekel, Shekelesh (or Sagalassans) and Weshesh. The inscription makes it clear that Greeks from the Aegean islands were involved (see below) but it is significant that the Akaiwasha (or Achaeans) were not included in the list of nations participating on this occasion.[15]

3 The Leadership of the "Migrations"

The Egyptian records of the time relating to the two major attacks on the Delta, referred to above, make it quite clear that, at least in one case, the attacks were made by a confederation of nations or tribes which was well directed by a strong and central leadership. This is clearly and specifically stated in the Egyptian inscription relating to the invasion of *c* 1192 B.C. which is transcribed by Hall in these words:[16]

> "*The Isles were restless,* disturbed among themselves at one and the same time. *No land stood before them beginning* from *Kheta,* Kedi (Cilicia), Carchemish, Arvad and *Alashiya.* They destroyed (them, and *assembled in their) camp in one place* in the midst of *Amor* (Amurru: Palestine). They desolated its people and its land like

> one which is not. They came with fire prepared before them, forward towards Egypt. Their main strength was (composed of) *Pulesti,* Tjakaray, Shakalsha, Daanau, and Uashasha. *These lands were united,* and they laid their hands upon the land as far as the Circle of the Earth. Their hearts were *confident, full of their plans.*" (The italics are mine.)

This inscription is a most valuable historical record as it shows that, apart from being under a confident, well-organized and central leadership, the attack came from the north, that the Greeks from the Isles were involved as well as the Pulesti (Philistines), that they overran amongst other places Kheta (the Hittite kingdom) and Alashiya (Cyprus) as they advanced southward to establish a central base in Amurru (Palestine). Ramesses III acted energetically and mounted an amphibious counterattack in which the Egyptian fleet (perhaps reinforced and inspired by refugee ships and their crews from the coasts of the eastern Mediterranean) was used skilfully in a manner apparently unknown in the Egyptian records before that time. This effort was successful both on land and sea as the inscription goes on to record that they were trapped like wild-fowl and that the Egyptian fleet took the invaders' ships by surprise in the "harbour-mouths", attacking them like "a full flame". In the words of Hall's transcription the record proceeds,

> "*those who reached my frontier,* their seed is not; their heart and soul are perished for ever. As for *those who assembled before them on the sea,* the full flame was in their front, *before the harbour-mouths,* and a wall of metal upon the shore surrounded them. They were dragged, capsized and laid low upon the beach; slain and made heaps . . ." (my italics.)

From this part of the Egyptian inscription we learn that the invaders reached the frontiers before they were defeated and the ships *that were with them* were destroyed.

In the historical section of the famous Papyrus Harris,[17] which commemorates the events of the reign of Ramesses III in a unique papyrus roll no less than 133 feet long, it is interesting to find that a clear distinction is drawn between the various groups which made up

"The Peoples of the Sea". The Danaans (Denyen) are described "as living in their isles" and the Sardinians (Sherden) as being "of the sea". In contrast the Teukrians (Thekel or Tjakaray) and Philistines (Peleset or Pulesti) are listed without qualification. From this it appears that at that time the Danaans were islanders, the Sardinians lived across the sea as did the Weshesh, presumably in contrast on mainland territory, while the Teukrians and Philistines were unqualified mainlanders. If, therefore, we are to attempt an identification of the Dorians from the Egyptian records we must look to the Sardinians or to the Weshesh, and to the Danaans as their island relatives, as tentative candidates at the time of these events.

The location of the battle has been interpreted as being at the "mouths" of the Pelusic Nile. Evidently the defeat, while decisive, was not overwhelming because the Pulesti, who were included in the defeated confederation, settled in Palestine in the area of the Shephelah and founded the nation of the Philistines there; while the Libyans three years later still felt that they could stage a further invasion of the western frontier of Egypt.[18] Perhaps the explanation of this can be found in other Egyptian texts dealing with the invasion of Palestine by Thothmes III. Referring to the famous battle of Megiddo (*c* 1479 B.C.), one text indicates:[19] "had not His Majesty's soldiers given their hearts to plundering the enemy's possessions they would have taken Megiddo at this moment", and in a second text dealing with Thothmes' fifth campaign after taking the coastal city of Arvad the scribe states:[20] "Behold! His Majesty's army was drunk and anointed with oil every day as at a feast in Egypt". Evidently the Egyptian armies were not very good at following up their victories at the crucial moment, which explains why "The Peoples of the Sea" survived to found, *inter alia,* the Philistine nation.

Recent authorities[21] have listed the following peoples as appearing in the lists of the raiders of the Delta recorded by the Egyptian scribes: Tursha (Tursenoi), Luka (Lycians), Peleset (Philistines), Akaiwasha (Achaeans—although *not* present at the invasion of *c* 1192), Denyen (Danaoi) and Meshwesh (Libyans). Although the various peoples cannot always be identified with absolute certainty, there can be no doubt that the Greeks, Trojans and their allies were present and probably formed the backbone of the movements.

Dealing with a somewhat later phase of the great migrations when, in the time of Tiglath Pileser I around the later part of the twelfth century B.C., the Muski (or Phrygians) were expanding southward, we find the Assyrian historical account quoted by Seton Lloyd:[22] "of how Tiglath Pileser I routed a Muski army of 20,000 men under five kings which had invaded northern Mesopotamia".

The invaders can be visualized as a confederation of well-organized nations and tribes similar to those described in the "Catalogues" of the *Iliad* for the Achaean and Trojan armies assembled respectively under Agamemnon "King of Men" and Priam "King of Troy". In both cases the historical record makes it clear that the invasions were not just spontaneous and haphazard migrations. This is not unexpected as in more recent historical periods for which we have detailed records, from Attila to Hitler, such invasions for plunder and conquest have usually been inspired and led by one man.

Because the Egyptian inscriptions at the temple of Medinet Habu are illustrated with pictorial scenes showing the invaders (*c* 1192 B.C.) accompanied by two-wheeled oxcarts in which are women and children, it has been inferred that "The Peoples of the Sea" were a migratory movement of tribes expelled by disturbances in the far north and seeking new lands for settlement. However, such refugees could hardly have made a head-on attack on the armed might of Egypt, and surely could have found fertile lands to settle further north. It is more likely that the oxcarts merely accompanied the invaders to carry their booty and captives, the women, children and slaves that they had gathered on their passage southwards.

4 Contacts between the Greeks and Hittites

The Hittite records have been described and analysed by O. R. Gurney[23] in an illuminating and thorough manner, and the following historical facts are significant for their contacts with the Greeks and Trojans:

c 1339–1282 B.C. From the "Tawagalawas letter"[24] probably dating from the reign of either Mursilis or Muwatallis we learn that Millawanda (Milawata or Miletus) owed allegiance to the king of Ahhiyawā. Also that the royal families of Ahhiyawā and Hatti were on terms of close, even intimate friendship.

c 1250 B.C. From the so called "Milawata letter",[25] which is known to be later than the "Tawagalawas letter", and may conceivably be dated around 1250 B.C. or later, we find that the ruler of Millawanda was claimed to be a vassal of the Hittite king.

c 1250–1220 B.C. From a letter[26] written by Tudhaliyas IV to a king of Amurru we learn that the king of Ahhiyawā (Achaea) was regarded as being one of the "Big Five" (Hatti, Achaea, Egypt, Babylon and Assyria), and there is evidence from the records that the friendship between the two countries was becoming strained.

c 1250–1220 B.C. From another fragmentary text,[27] ascribed to the reign of Tudhaliyas IV, we have confirmation that the king of Ahhiyawā at that time had been present in Asia Minor in person, had been encroaching on the Hittite preserves in the land of the Seha River and had been forced to withdraw.

c 1250–1220 B.C. A list of towns and districts[28] occurring in one of the Hittite texts, which lists the geographical locations working from south to north, starting with the "Lukka Lands" (Lycia) and finishing with Assuwa, mentions the names of two places: Ta-ru-(u)-i-ša and U-i-lu-ši-ia. These two names have been identified with Troy and Ilios respectively, and one of the Hittite texts records that at the time of Muwatallis (king of the Hittites during the period *c* 1300 B.C.), the vassal king of Wilusa was Alaksandrus. As Gurney comments: "The reader cannot fail to be struck by the resemblance of this name to Alexandros (alias Paris) the prince of Ilios (Troy)".

c 1250–1190 B.C. The activities of Attarissiyas, referred to as "a man of Ahhiyā", began in the borderlands of Hatti during the reign of Tudhaliyas IV[27] (*c* 1250 to 1220 B.C.) and continued after the latter's death *c* 1220 B.C. through into the reign of Arnuwandus III. At that time Attarissiyas was defeated in battle by the Hittite king.

c 1190 B.C. The Hittite records cease abruptly, and we must assume that this date marks the overrunning of the Hittite empire by invasion from the north.

For further details Gurney's interesting analysis of these texts may be referred to, and the point is made that there are a number of discrepancies. However, as in the case of identifying the Ahhiyawā folk with the Achaeans, these interpretations can certainly be accepted as a working hypothesis, and Desborough[29] regards it as probable that the kingdom of Ahhiyawā should be identified with the Mycenaean empire ruled over by a king centred at Mycenae.

5 *The "Big Five"*

The Hittite text of the Tawagalawas letter refers to the messenger bearing it as: "a man of some importance; he is the groom who has ridden with me in my chariot from my youth up, and not only with me but also with your brother and with Tawagalawas". As Gurney points out:[24]

> "Here is evidence of a very close, even intimate, relationship at one time between Hatti and Ahhiyawā, or at least between their royal families. Indeed the whole tenor of the letter is friendly and respectful."

These interpretations of the Hittite records have received increasing support in recent years and Hammond[30] refers as follows to the Hittite letter:

> "... which asked for help against invaders, a Hittite king's 'brother' (that is a king of similar standing), called 'Tavakavalas', was described as being an 'Ayavalash' king and a 'brother' of the king of 'Ahhiyava' ... The word 'Ahhiyava' (or in its earliest form 'Ahhiyiva') is clearly a transcription of the Greek word 'Akhaia', just as 'Ayavalash' (of which the ending is a Hittite ethnic) is a transcription of 'Akhaios'. There were evidently two Achaean kings in the earlier letter: one being the king of Achaea par excellence, as in the later letter, and comparable in status with the kings of Egypt, &c., and the other some local Achaean king in Asia Minor. The former was evidently a king of the Greek mainland. The clue to the latter is probably given by Herodotus, who mentioned that the inhabitants of Pamphylia or Cilicia were once called 'Hyp-Akhaioi'. 'Lazpa' was doubtless the island Lesbos, and 'Taroisa' (in another Hittite document) was Troy."

Desborough[29] states his belief in a Mycenaean empire which clashed with the Hittites on the west coast of Asia Minor and which can be identified with the Ahhiyawa mentioned in the Hittite tablets.

The thesis that there were political contacts between the Grecian mainland and Egypt finds striking confirmation in the recent publication by Kitchen of a honorific inscription on the base of one of the statues in the funeral temple of Amenhotep III (1406–1369 B.C.) at Kom el Hetan. As analysed further by Astour[31] the nine place names recorded can be allocated: four to the kingdom of Pylos (the district of Na-pe-re-wa, Me-za-na, the Messena of classical times, Wa-e-ro, and the important town of Pa-ki-ja-ne), four to Crete (Knossos, Amnisos, Lyktos and Dikte, near which was the Cretan city of Diktaia), and finally one to the island of Cythera itself, on the route between Pylos and the island of Crete, where traces of early contacts with Egypt and Asia Minor had already been found. It was the Egyptian custom to record such honorific inscriptions in order to give the impression that the places mentioned were tributary to Egypt. In many cases the correct interpretation is that they were important enough to make it desirable that the impression should be created, rather than that the Egyptian rule extended to such areas.

These conclusions are consistent with the Greek tradition of a "Thalassocracy", and it is generally recognized that from the capture of Knossos by the Mycenaeans *c* 1450 B.C. until about the time of the Dorian invasion in the twelfth century B.C. the command of the seas, at least in the Aegean and eastern Mediterranean, was in the hands of the Mainland Greeks. Presumably these were a confederation headed by the king of Mycenae and included Crete. The Mycenaeans also fell heir to other Minoan possessions. Tradition claims that the Achaean "Minos" suppressed the Carian pirates[32] and that his brothers Sarpedon and Rhadamanthys colonized the coastal areas of Caria and Lycia. Some confirmation of this legend has now been found as it has been established that at Miletus the original settlers came from Crete, and in the strata from about the date of the fall of Knossos Mycenaean remains begin to be found. The same is true for Phylakopi on Melos.[33]

In Rhodes archaeology has confirmed[34] that the Minoan settlement near the village of Trianda was suddenly deserted *c* 1410 B.C., having previously coexisted peaceably with the nearby Mycenaean settlement at Ialysos. Palmer quotes Stubbings as concluding that: ". . . this must mean that after the fall of the Minoan central power the Rhodian outpost underwent the same fate".

In Cyprus the Minoans had trading relations but apparently no settlements. However, the Mycenaeans seem to have established themselves there, possibly expanding southwards from Rhodes, and the rich "House of Bronzes" found at Enkomi may have been that of the Mycenaean governor.

On the mainland of Asia Minor Mycenaean remains occur at Miletus and at sites in Cilicia, some of which were destroyed by "The Peoples of the Sea" *c* 1200 B.C.[35] At Tarsus[36] the settlement, which had been under Hittite domination, was destroyed possibly after the reign of the Hittite king Hattusilis III (died *c* 1250 B.C.) and was rebuilt, the re-occupiers being Mycenaeans. At Miletus there was a definite fortified Mycenaean settlement in this period. The fortification wall is very like Mycenaean work and seems to have been built in the second half of the thirteenth century B.C.,[37] later than the Milawata letter, i.e. after the fall of Troy. There is also evidence of Mycenaean influence, if not in some cases settlements, in Syria[38] at Atchana, Ras Shamra (Ugarit) and Tell Sukas, all of which were destroyed by "The Peoples of the Sea" *c* 1200 B.C.

In recent years more discoveries of Mycenaean deposits in these areas have become known, one of the latest being that reported by Bass, of the University Museum of the University of Pennsylvania, who records the finding in 1963 of fine examples of Mycenaean pottery at Muskebi on the west coast of Turkey near Halicarnassus. He reports that these finds may date back to a period between 1400 and 1100 B.C.

The Mycenaean/Trojan power in the Aegean basin was therefore a powerful one, comparable with the other major contemporary powers. The *Iliad* confirms this pattern of a confederation of Greek kingdoms owing allegiance to Agamemnon, the king of Mycenae. The situation may be compared with France in the early Middle Ages, when at times the writ of the king hardly ran beyond the confines of Paris, though he was the feudal head of a powerful confederation of dukedoms and kingdoms which, in time of war, would unite together under him. Even the position of Millawanda is paralleled by that of provinces on the English marches, such as Aquitania, which at different times owed allegiance either to France or England, sometimes even to both. The paradox could therefore arise of the king of England owing homage to the king of France for a French province in his own possession.

6 Summary of the Historical Record

1. Pylos fell, presumably to the "Dorians", during the same period (*c* 1200 B.C.) as the fall of Hatti (*c* 1190 B.C.) and the attempted invasion of Egypt (*c.* 1192 B.C.). These dates can all be taken as contemporaneous and not necessarily as indicating the exact order of these events.
2. "The Peoples of the Sea" who invaded Egypt came from the north and included Greek and Trojan nations and tribes owing allegiance to them. The invasion of *c* 1221 B.C. included Achaeans who were not listed amongst the attackers of the latest invasion in 1192, though this did include the Danaoi.
3. "The Peoples of the Sea" were strongly and centrally led, and were not just a spontaneous and inchoate migration.
4. The Greeks and the Trojans were in close contact with the Hittite empire, and after the fall of Troy—accepting Blegen's date of *c* 1250 B.C.—the friendly relations between the Achaean (or Mycenaean) kings and the rulers of Hatti became first strained and then hostile.
5. The Mycenaean confederation was an important power in the Aegean, and the king of Mycenae ranked as one of the "Big Five". After the fall of Troy this influence expanded into the mainland coastal regions of Asia Minor and Syria.

A considerable body of archaeological evidence is still growing as the results accumulate from new excavations and from the re-interpretation of older data in the light of new evidence and techniques. There is also a mass of Greek tradition interwoven with a rich thread of Bardic legend. In the following chapter a number of theories will be developed from these historical, archaeological and traditional sources in order to relate the Dorian invasions to other contemporary events in the eastern Mediterranean.

REFERENCES

[1] Palmer, L. R., *Mycenaeans and Minoans,* 1961, p. 133.
[2] Palmer, L. R., *ibid,* p. 140f.

[3] Palmer, L. R., *ibid*, p. 134.
[4] Palmer, L. R., *ibid*, p. 139.
[5] Palmer, L. R., *ibid*, p. 103.
[6] Palmer, L. R., *ibid*, p. 142f.
[7] Thucydides, *The Peloponnesian War*, Bantam Classic, 1960, Book IV, p. 233.
[8] Palmer, L. R., *ibid*, p. 149f.
[9] Blegen, C. W., *Troy and the Trojans*, 1963, p. 163.
[10] Hammond, N. G. L., *A History of Greece to 322 B.C.*, 1959, p. 75.
[11] Palmer, L. R., *ibid*, p. 149.
[12] Gurney, O. R., *The Hittites*, Pelican Books, 1961, p. 35.
[13] Hammond, N. G. L., *ibid*, p. 52.
[14] Hammond, N. G. L., *ibid*, p. 53.
[15] Hutchinson, R. W., *Prehistoric Crete*, Pelican Books, 1962, p. 315.
[16] Hall, H. R., *The Ancient History of the Near East*, 1960, p. 380f.
[17] Breasted, J. H., *Ancient Records of Egypt*, The University of Chicago Press, 1906, Volume IV, p. 201.
[18] Hall, H. R., *ibid*, p. 383.
[19] Hall, H. R., *ibid*, p. 238.
[20] Hall, H. R., *ibid*, p. 240.
[21] Hammond, N. G. L., *ibid*, p. 73.
[22] Seton Lloyd, *Early Anatolia*, Pelican Books, 1956, p. 191.
[23] Gurney, O. R., *ibid*, pp. 46–58.
[24] Gurney, O. R., *ibid*, p. 49.
[25] Gurney, O. R., *ibid*, p. 50.
[26] Gurney, O. R., *ibid*, p. 50f.
[27] Gurney, O. R., *ibid*, p. 51.
[28] Gurney, O. R., *ibid*, p. 56f.
[29] Desborough, V. R. d'A., *The Last Mycenaeans and their Successors*, 1964, p. 219f.
[30] Hammond, N. G. L., *ibid*, p. 51.
[31] Astour, Michael C., American Journal of Archaeology, 70, 1966, p. 313f.
[32] Gurney, O. R., *ibid*, p. 56.
[33] Desborough, V. R. d'A., *ibid*, p. 162; MacKendrick, P., *The Greek Stones Speak*, 1962, p. 132.
[34] Palmer, L. R., *ibid*, p. 211.
[35] Hammond, N. G. L., *ibid*, p. 63.
[36] Desborough, V. R. d'A., *ibid*, p. 205.
[37] Desborough, V. R. d'A., *ibid*, p. 220.
[38] Desborough, V. R. d'A., *ibid*, p. 207f.

CHAPTER THREE

The Theories

I disapprove of what you say, but I will
defend to the death your right to say it

VOLTAIRE

AN examination of the historical background outlined in Chapter 2, together with relevant Greek traditions and archaeological information, may help to determine to what extent they are interrelated and whether this approach to the problem throws any light on the mystery of the Dorian invasions. Around 1200 B.C. three major events occurred: most of the Mycenaean kingdoms were destroyed, the Hittite empire was overrun, and there was a large-scale attack on the eastern Egyptian borders by "The Peoples of the Sea". Greeks were involved in all three events; in the first on the evidence of Greek tradition, supported by some additional evidence as we shall see in Chapter 6; and in the other two on the authority of contemporary Egyptian inscriptions, which include Greeks amongst the nations listed as making up "The Peoples of the Sea" and state that they overran Hatti in their southward march. It is reasonable to assume that these three events were in some way interrelated. The Egyptian scribes state quite clearly, referring to the origin of the attack: "The Isles were restless, disturbed amongst themselves at one and the same time." This could be interpreted as stating, in a particularly apt way, that the region of the northern "Isles", or Mycenaean empire, was engaged in a civil war or internal struggle for power and that the invasion arose out of this. There seems to be some evidence for such a Greek "Wars of the Roses", and this is dealt with later (Chapter 6). It is generally recognized, too, that the Mycenaean empire did defeat the Trojans and, on the evidence of the Hittite tablets, became active in Asia Minor. Indeed the Mycenaeans founded settlements and dynasties in areas which had previously been within the Trojan sphere of influence (Chapter 7).

The "Dorians", led by the Heracleidae, were enemies of the central Mycenaean power, and at the time of the Trojan War were traditionally settled in northern Thessaly and Macedonia. This area included the plain through which the river Axios flowed, and its inhabitants are included in Homer's Catalogue of the Trojan allies in the *Iliad*. The Trojan City, captured by the Mycenaeans *c* 1250 B.C., fell once more *c* 1200 B.C., but this time without destruction. It is reasonable to infer (Chapter 7) that it was liberated by the Dorians, whose previous frontal attack on Mycenae had failed when they were repulsed and their leader, Hyllus, slain.

The Egyptian inscriptions include the Greeks in both invasions, but the Achaeans in the first invasion only, *c* 1221 B.C. The Egyptian record states of the second invasion by "The Peoples of the Sea" that there was dissension in the Greek realms in the Aegean, that the invaders overcame Hatti, Kizzuwatna (Cilicia) and Cyprus; and we know from the archaeological record that Troy was "liberated" about this time. So the attack clearly came from the north, and the trail followed by the marching armies is identified by the written record. There is evidence that the invaders were supported by the "Greek" and "Trojan" nations present in Asia Minor, such as the Dardanians and Philistines. The route from the north is supported by the archaeological evidence that there was *no* destruction at this period in the Greek islands, nor in the Dodecanese (which probably supported the invaders). This indicates that the attack did not come from the west, i.e. from the Mycenaean empire itself, and this is confirmed by the absence of any reference to the Achaeans in the Egyptian records referring to this invasion. To mount an attack capable of liberating Troy, crushing the Hittite empire and overrunning Asia Minor and beyond to the Egyptian borders called for a relatively powerful nation. The only known candidates for this role are the "Dorians" who, we know, were capable of smashing the Mycenaean empire, and who lived at this time in the geographical area indicated as the source of the attack by "The Peoples of the Sea" *c* 1192 B.C. In fact it can be deduced that it was the wealth and armaments seized by the Dorians in this successful march southward through Asia Minor which, added to their manpower, put them in the position to crush the Mycenaean empire. We deduce, therefore, that "The Peoples of the Sea" in the first invasion of *c* 1221 B.C. can be equated with the Achaeans, and in the second invasion of *c* 1192 B.C. with the Dorians.

The weakened Hittite empire presented a tempting prize to the invaders and the historical record shows that it fell to invaders from the north. This success would have provided the wealth and armaments necessary to make them a considerable fighting force. The repulse of the subsequent raid on Egypt set the scene for the "return" of the Dorians, taking the normal sea-route from the coasts of Syria and Asia Minor to Greece, which ran through the island chain of Rhodes, Carpathos, Casos and Crete. The ensuing raid on Pylos—the soft underbelly of the Mycenaean confederation—proved successful and, turned into an occupation, was combined with an attack from the north, substantially along the traditional invasion route of the Dorians. This led to the subjugation of the Peloponnese and of the Mycenaean kingdoms in it.

To make the issue clear-cut I propose to state more detailed conclusions based on this general approach in the form of seven basic theories:

1. That the *initial* invasion of the Greek kingdoms by the Dorians did not come directly from the north but was a seaborne attack on Pylos carried out by the Dorian element of "The Peoples of the Sea" after they were repulsed from the Egyptian frontiers *c* 1192 B.C.

2. That the Dorians were Mycenaeans, or at least "fringe" Mycenaeans, who came from the north—Thessaly and Macedonia—drawing on less civilized northern peoples for manpower.

3. That the traditional attack on the Peloponnese by the Dorians, from the north via the Gulf of Corinth, reinforced the seaborne attack on Pylos and took place either simultaneously or shortly after.

4. That the Dorian invasion of Pylos was probably preceded by an attack on Crete, and on Knossos in particular, which was used temporarily as an invasion base, but not then permanently occupied. The occupation of Crete took place later, after the conquest of the Peloponnese, the Dorians setting out from there for the purpose, as traditionally recorded.

5. That after this successful invasion of the Peloponnese, these regions were swept by an outbreak of plague, which would account for the

extensive depopulation of the area. It would undoubtedly have spread also to adjacent areas such as Athens.

6. That after the depopulation by war, plague and probably famine, the Dorians progressively lost their control of the situation in the ensuing chaos. Ultimately, at least partly, the less civilized northern element of their subjects and allies inherited or seized control of extensive areas of their conquests.

7. That possibly the events recorded by Greek tradition, relating to the fall of Thebes, the siege of Troy and the Dorian migrations and conquests, were part of a Greek "Wars of the Roses" in which broadly the north and east were engaged against the south and south-west. The lines of this struggle were drawn roughly, but with fluctuations, as described in the "Catalogues" of the Achaean and Trojan forces recorded in the *Iliad*, with the Dorians as the final arbiters.

It is proposed to deal primarily with the first theory, but the part played by Crete in these events (Theory 4) is an important subsidiary question, particularly in the light of current controversies. The problem is as follows: "Did the Dorians invade Crete from the Grecian mainland, after overrunning it, or did they first attack it from Asia Minor, probably after the failure of the Egyptian invasion, and did Crete then act as the springboard for the invasion of the Greek mainland?" In Chapter 4 the conclusion is reached, after examination of the evidence, that very probably the *initial* invasion of the mainland did not come directly from the north but from Asia Minor via Crete, and that probably the invasion of Crete acted as a springboard for that invasion (Chapter 5). This theory is, of course, not vital to the main theory; it is developed further in Chapter 5.

That the Mycenaean (or Achaean) empire was regarded in the thirteenth century B.C. as one of the "Big Five" (Mycenae, Hatti, Egypt, Assyria, Babylon), and that the friendly relationship which existed with the Hittite kingdom in the time of Mursilis/Muwatallis had degenerated into rivalry and friction by the time of Tudhaliyas IV, is a matter of history recorded contemporaneously in the Hittite royal archives. The details of this story have been ably dealt with by Gurney,[1] as summarized in Chapter 2. It appears likely from the records that the Mycenaean hegemony extended to some of the islands and provinces of the Asia Minor coast, partly as an inheritance from the Minoan empire, and it is also possible that Troy was a member of the Mycenaean confederation, however loosely so. Some authorities have definitely linked the Achaeans with the Ahhiyawans, and at this time Mycenae was believed to head the Achaean confederation of Greek states. Both the Mycenaeans (Greeks and their Trojan allies) and the Hittites were faced with the same problem: they were potentially threatened from the north by the warlike and less civilized nations occupying a wide arc north of the Hellespont, specifically by the "Dorians" in the case of the Greek kingdoms. These peoples—from the time of the Minyans to the Dorians and beyond—naturally regarded the rich and civilized lands to the south with greed and envy, and periodically raided or invaded Asia Minor to loot, burn and even settle. This threat was particularly serious for the Hittites, who throughout their history were obliged to engage in war on more than one front. Indeed this ultimately led to the disintegration of their empire about 1200–1190 B.C. when they were overrun from the north-west.

The strategic key to this situation was Troy, which commanded one of the most important invasion routes into Asia Minor, so that co-operation between the Hittite empire and the Mycenaean and Trojan nations was logical and natural. This would have been the case particularly if Troy had also been a member of the Mycenaean confederation, though this is not essential, as the same would hold true if she had been allied to, or even only friendly with, the Mycenaean kingdom. At least the Mycenaean interest lay directly in keeping open the trade-routes from which prosperity was derived, and in avoiding a threat to the lines of communication with their customers and trading-posts on the coasts of the Black Sea and Asia Minor.

In view of the Mycenaean thalassocracy, which Greek traditions from the Classical Age claimed existed (and this is now widely accepted as fact), it is logical to assume that an alliance with Troy would have been maintained, at least initially, to enable the Mycenaeans to keep open their trade-routes to the Black Sea. From the Hittite royal archives we have seen that some event occurred which destroyed the good relations between the Achaeans and Hittites. This may well be connected with the breakdown of the coexistence or alliance between Troy and the Mycenaean confederation. This will be further discussed in Chapter 6. The eventual outcome was a war between the two

Aegean powers, ending with the victory of the Mycenaean faction and the fall of Troy.

The aftermath of this event is discussed later (Chapter 7), but it is enough to postulate here that the immediate result of the fall of Troy was the extension of Mycenaean influence in the area. This would have extended beyond Troy itself to the more desirable territories of its allied neighbours and the weaker of the nearby settlements. This situation can best be described in Hammond's comment:[2]

> "The returns (nostoi) of the Achaeans from Troy were recorded in the epic saga. During the sea-raids many chieftains with their heterogeneous following carved out new kingdoms for themselves. In Cyprus they established dynasties at Paphus, Salamis, Curium, Lapathus and Soli, which traced their descent from leading families of Mycenaean Arcadia, Salamis, Argolis, Laconia and Attica. Archaeological evidence of intrusion in the latest phase of the Bronze Age has recently been found at Sinda in Central Cyprus. There they reinforced the earlier Mycenaean settlers, over whom Cinyras was king at the time of the Trojan War, and dynasties representing both waves of settlement survived into classical times, the Cinyradae at Paphus, for instance, and the Teucridae at Salamis. On the south coast of Asia Minor Achaeans, Cilicians and Pamphylians came from the Troad to found new settlements. The Achaean leaders, including Amphilochus of Argos, Calchas of Mycenae, and Mopsus of Thebes, planted settlements at Phaselis, Olbia, Aspendus, Selge, Soli, Tarsus, Mallus, and on the Syrian coast at Poseidium . . ."

We have in fact a perfect picture of the operation of the Indo-European feudal system, familiar to us as it continued into our own Middle Ages, in which the king's chief supporters, and the younger sons of noble families, carved out new centres of power for themselves; forming these "colonies" by settling in and seizing power as the new local dynasty. The new leader normally brought with him only his own elite bodyguard and supporters. This is exactly what one would have expected after the fall of Troy and the collapse of the Trojan confederation.

One striking example of this type of infiltration, after the fall of

Troy, is quoted by Herodotus. He records that the Heraclids ruled Lydia for 22 generations, lasting over a period of 505 years, before the family of Croesus—the Mermnadae—took over, and gives a detailed list of the kings of that house whose reigns total 170 years down to the fall of Croesus, which is dated historically as 546 B.C.[3] From these data we can reconstruct the date at which the Heraclids seized power in Lydia and we arrive at the figure of 1221 B.C. It should be recalled that Herodotus was a native of Halicarnassus, bordering on Lydia, and therefore ideally placed to check and record the genealogies of the Lydian kings for the period we are considering. It is greatly to his credit that in this case he is quite specific with regard to the names at both ends of the genealogies in question, and quotes the time periods in years rather than in generations.

The exact coincidence of this date for the founding of the Mycenaean royal house in Lydia with that for the invasion of Egypt in 1221 B.C., in which the Achaeans participated according to the Egyptian records, is probably fortuitous, but it is remarkable that it falls in the right period. Herodotus uses a delightful euphemism for the "take-over", in which he describes how the Lydian princes: ". . . turned over the management of affairs to the Heraclids." In the generation following the fall of Troy, when the Mycenaean power was expanding southwards, we can well imagine a situation similar to that which prevailed in England following the Norman conquest, when lands and fiefdoms were taken over by forcible persuasion or by the marriage of the leaders of the conquerors with the Saxon heiresses.

The archaeological evidence from the coasts of Asia Minor gives some support to this record by Herodotus. We do not, of course, know the extent of the Lydian kingdom at this time, but it was presumably centred round the coastal arc bounded on the north by Chios and on the south by Samos. Miletus may even have been included, but if not it would have pertained to the Carians, who were kinsmen of the Lydians and may well have joined with them in the expeditions of "The Peoples of the Sea", as is witnessed by the Carian head-dresses featured in the Egyptian records of these events. In Desborough's survey[4] of this area he expresses the view that Samos came within the range of Mycenaean influence, and that recent excavations at Emborio, on the south coast of Chios, show few signs of

Mycenaean settlement in the LH IIIb period (i.e. prior to *c* 1230 B.C.) but definite evidence of a settlement in the succeeding LH IIIc period. Regarding Miletus he reports that there was no evidence of any violent interruption at the end of the LH IIIb period, and that LH IIIc material is well represented. The *later* LH IIIc destruction of the city was followed by a re-occupation characterized by sub-Mycenaean and Proto-geometric sherds, and the opinion is expressed that the interval between destruction and re-occupation need not have been great. It would seem that we could safely assume that the destruction of the city took place after the passage of "The Peoples of the Sea" *c* 1200 B.C. Machteld J. Mellink has also expressed the view that the old city of Ephesus is finally yielding some corroboration for the theory that it was an active participant in the Ahhiyava age.

There is also evidence that the Mycenaeans controlled Colophon, whose site, with a towering Acropolis dominating the rich plain below, has been described as strikingly similar to those chosen for major Mycenaean cities on the Greek mainland. Here it is worth recalling the tradition relating to Colophon that the earliest Ionian invaders (*c* 1000 B.C.) came to terms with the inhabitants of the city, described as *Cretans* and *Cadmeians,* who in their turn had displaced the indigenous Carians who previously occupied this area. The presence of Cretans here is understandable, for instance as the descendants of refugees from eastern Crete after the devastation of Zakros and other centres—as the result of the volcanic disaster at the island of Thera (Chapter 5)—or from the Mycenaean invasion which followed, as well as mercenaries and immigrants who had participated in the Minoan and Mycenaean expansion into the area.

If the theory is correct that Thebes as well as Thessaly took sides with the Dorians in the last stages of this Grecian "Wars of the Roses" (Chapter 6), their subsequent presence in Lydia is also not unexpected. If the legend is correct that the Heraclids assumed power in Lydia after the fall of Troy, and retained it for more than 500 years thereafter, it would be quite natural for parties of Cadmeians from Thebes to join up with them. The Heraclids could thus have obtained the feudal power they needed to hold the Lydian throne in the disturbed times which followed the fall of Troy, and the passage of "The Peoples of the Sea" about 1200 B.C. The archaeological evidence as well as legend indicate that Mycenaean power and influence increased in these areas in the coasts of Asia Minor following the fall of Troy, and persisted there after the passages of "The Peoples of the Sea". The indication, if not positive proof, that centres such as Miletus were not destroyed at that time lends weight to the theory that "The Peoples of the Sea" were not just barbaric hordes from the north, but that on the second occasion (*c* 1200 B.C.) they were Dorians led by the Heraclids and allied with the peoples of the old Trojan confederation. Otherwise another explanation has to be found for the fact that these centres were not sacked at that time.

With the dwindling of Mycenaean power on the mainland caused by the dissensions accentuated by the Trojan War, and the consolidation of Heraclid rule in Rhodes and Lydia, the stage was set for the latter to join forces with their kinsmen who were leaders of the Dorians. Thus all the necessary elements were present for a successful revolt against the central Mycenaean power on the coasts of Asia Minor, and for further adventures against Hatti and to the south towards Egypt.

We now turn to the first of the two main invasions of Egypt by "The Peoples of the Sea", which took place *c* 1221 B.C. in alliance with the Libyans. This invasion could have been partly inspired by the Mycenaean condottiere and their descendants, in search of further plunder, particularly leaders such as the Attarissayas of the Hittite records and the legendary Amphilochus[5] of Poseidium (the port of al Mina plus the hill-town of Sabouni) where Mycenaean sherds of the thirteenth and twelfth centuries B.C. have been found. It appears likely that the suzerainty of the king of Mycenae extended over many of these areas, however loosely, as the Hittite records make it clear that Attarissayas,[6] who operated around 1220 B.C., was a "man of Ahhiya" (see Chapter 2). But the attack on Egypt could have happened with or without the connivance of the Mycenaean "High King", much as in Elizabethan times Drake and other freebooter captains attacked and sacked Spanish settlements without a state of war officially existing.

This raid was repulsed decisively, and the Egyptian records show that as well as the Achaeans (Akaiwasha) who played a prominent part (see Chapter 2), some of the others such as the Luka (Lycians), Dardanians and Peleset (Philistines) can be identified with peoples who came under Mycenaean influence after Troy fell. In the attack on the western borders of Egypt, those who were not slain or taken prisoner must mostly have returned to their respective homelands. This defeat would seriously have weakened the Mycenaean hold in Asia Minor. This was doubtless already stretched to the limit, by the usurpation of the Trojan sphere of influence and by the subsequent clashes with the Hittites (see Chapter 2). These clashes must also have undermined the Hittite empire, weakened as it already was by the strain of the Egyptian wars, culminating in the Pyrrhic victory of Kadesh (*c* 1285 B.C.), and the national effort needed to drive out the wild Kaskan tribesmen who had sacked the capital of Hattusas[7] while the Hittite power was concentrated on the southern borders to deal with the Egyptian crisis and to maintain the borders facing Babylonia.

The stage was thus set for the fall of the Hittite empire, and for the second major invasion of "The Peoples of the Sea", which this time, according to our theory, included those nations known to later Greek tradition as the "Dorians". A complete collapse occurred with far-reaching consequences: not only the Hittite empire, but undoubtedly any newly-founded dynasties set up by the Mycenaeans after the fall of Troy must also have been submerged by the invading armies from the north. Possibly they may sometimes have joined in alliance with the invasion leaders. It must be remembered that the local inhabitants, specifically the Trojans and their allies, would have looked upon the Dorian invaders as liberators from the Mycenaean yoke. Indeed, they would partly have welcomed them as their former allies. Certainly the archaeological record from Troy indicates this (see Chapter 7), since at this time (*c* 1200 B.C.) the city was not burnt and the intruders seem to have settled down side by side with the inhabitants.

We shall probably never know the exact causes of the fall of Hatti. Possibly it was due to a serious weakening of national manpower, resulting from the attrition of wars and famine in the previous two or three generations, and the employment of unreliable mercenaries to fill the gap; or to the weakness of the rulers following Tudhaliyas IV, or to the dissatisfaction with living conditions of the Hittite masses and their subject peoples. Very likely it was a combination of all these; but the result is clear: the Hittite empire vanished.

Like Gaul, its remnants seem to have been divided into three parts.

The first, comprising the main Hittite kingdom centred on Hattusas, was ultimately taken over by the Muski[8] (classical Moschi), generally identified with the Phrygians.[9] Their homeland was Thrace, according to Greek tradition, and by the time of the Trojan War they were already neighbours of the Trojans, if we accept the story of the *Iliad*. The Assyrian records of the time of Tiglath Pileser I, in the twelfth century B.C., quoted by Seton Lloyd,[10] relate how the Assyrian king routed a "Muski" army of 20,000 men under five kings which had invaded northern Mesopotamia. There is then a lapse of 200 years until the ninth century, when there is a further Assyrian reference to the "Muski", who can now definitely be identified with the Phrygians of Greek tradition, and understood to have founded a state on the debris of the Hittite empire.

The second portion, the south-western Hittite provinces, survived for no less that five centuries as the Neo-Hittite kingdoms. Here the situation can be summed up in Gurney's words:[11]

> "Assyrian records continue to refer to the Taurus area and Syria as the 'Land of Hatti . . .' All this proves that the traditions of Hittite culture were perpetuated from Malatya to the borders of Palestine down to the time when all that area became part of the empire of Assyria . . . It seems that Syria must have been overrun by another people coming from one of the Hittite provinces who had adopted the Hittite civilization . . . it is suggested that the province in question was that of Kizzuwatna. This was no organized invasion under a single leader . . ."

The last part comprises the areas bordering the Mediterranean which, even if not Hittite provinces, at least acknowledged Hittite suzerainty. Archaeological evidence here shows widespread destruction. Mersin and Atchana, to mention some of the most important, were destroyed then (*c* 1200 B.C.).

A recent report[12] of the decipherment of a text from Alasija, drawn up in the reign of Suppiluliumas II, describes a sea battle off Alasija *c* 1180 B.C., and how the king's forces beat back the ships of the raiders and levied a tribute of copper and gold on Cyprus. After the victory the Hittite king dedicated a temple and a statue to his father Tudhaliyas IV. If this date of *c* 1180 is taken in relation to the generally accepted one of *c* 1190 B.C. for the fall of the capital of the Hittite empire at Boghazkoy it would appear that, when the Hittite empire was overrun by "The Peoples of the Sea", the ruling power was forced southwards, and was able ultimately to re-establish itself in the area which became the Neo-Hittite kingdoms. If the text can be fully believed the Hittites, after the return of "The Peoples of the Sea", were even able to assert some temporary measure of control over Cyprus, which is in line with the fact that the island did not remain Dorian. It was after this battle that Enkomi revived again, presumably with the previous Mycenaean occupants in control. From this account Egypt does not appear to be a significant factor any more, otherwise we should find it hard to reconcile the survival of Hittite rule in this area, and the establishment of Philistine domination further south, with a powerful Egypt. Evidently the decline which culminated in the period of the Ramessides had already begun.

The historical and archaeological evidence does suggest an invasion from the northwest across the land-bridges of the Hellespont and possibly the Bosporus, then splitting into two streams. The first, the Muski (or Phrygians), overran the Hittite homeland, and partly displaced them southward into the areas protected by the Taurus mountains. These ultimately became the Neo-Hittite kingdoms and states when the disturbance of the invasion had subsided. The second stream comprised "The Peoples of the Sea", who overran Troy and the coastal areas and then pressed on southward towards Egypt.

The Egyptians record "The Peoples of the Sea" as flooding down the Syrian coasts, with wagons loaded with plunder and captives whilst their fleet kept pace with their right flank. The confident mood of this invasion can be imagined. Egypt was apparently in a state of decline: only a few decades before the Hittites had repulsed Ramesses II at Kadesh,[13] while they in their turn had crushed the mighty Hittite empire and swept irresistibly forward over all the intervening kingdoms from Troy to Syria and beyond. Egypt was a tempting prize, noted as the land richest in gold in the known world, and the wealth of the country must have seemed plunder almost within grasp. Egyptian records indicate a strong and central leadership for the invasion, and the manpower available must have been swollen by the disbanded armies of Hatti and the other kingdoms overrun. These forces would have been armed from the Hittite war-stores captured by the invaders. All the conditions seemed made for success, but with commendable energy the Egyptians under Ramesses III mounted a rapid counter-attack, using seapower and land forces to fall upon the invaders simultaneously. Possibly the Egyptians had incorporated in their fleet ships from Cyprus and the various maritime nations along the eastern Mediterranean which had fled southwards before the invaders. Perhaps their captains provided the idea and the means for mounting this amphibious counter-offensive.

The Egyptian inscriptions claim an overwhelming victory for themselves, but we have only their account (see Chapter 2). Their rulers, as many other leaders in more recent historical times, were prone to exaggerate; Ramesses II was guilty of this after the battle of Kadesh (*c* 1285 B.C.). Subsequent events showed there had been no overwhelming victory over the Hittites. Indeed Ramesses II escaped complete disaster only after coming very near to it.[13]

It is clear that the Egyptians did not now take advantage of the power vacuum created by the fall of the Hittite empire to occupy all the kingdoms, practically up to the Taurus mountains, which had been in dispute between these two great powers during the preceding centuries. Whether this failure was due to their victory being less complete than claimed or to the exhaustion of their empire, we shall probably never know.

This brings us to the crux of the matter: "What happened to 'The Peoples of the Sea' after this repulse?" Whether the defeat was partial or merely a defeat of the advance guard, it is most probable that many of the invaders survived, as well as their allies. The area they had conquered, stretching back to Troy, must have held large numbers of occupying troops and reinforcements pressing on to join the attack on Egypt. That many survived the main battle receives strong support from two incidents referred to in Chapter 2. These show the Egyptian troops did not always press home their victories. After this defeat, when the various peoples were left stranded and displaced from their original homes, the Peleset or Philistines settled in the Shephelah region of Palestine and no doubt incorporated other masterless men originating from the Mycenaean settlements in the eastern Mediterranean.

Tradition claims that the Philistines were of Cretan and Lycian origin, and for some time it has been clear that their culture had close connections with some Mycenaean source, because of the close resemblance of their characteristic "Philistine Ware" to pottery of the LH IIIc period from the Argolid and Attica. This Philistine Ware is found abundantly in those areas of southern Palestine which the Bible refers to as Philistine strongholds. More recently further evidence has been coming forward which reinforces the conclusions drawn from their pottery. On the one hand Dothan[14] describes cult objects excavated from the Philistine cemetery at Azor, and from the stratified site of Ashdod which features in biblical accounts of this people. Amongst these cult objects we find figurines of numerous "mourning women" and of a "mother goddess, enthroned". The former occur both free-standing and forming part of the adornment of kraters, almost certainly used in ceremonial burials, in which the "mourning women" and small cups are alternated as attachments to the rim of the krater. This arrangement, unique in Palestine, has close parallels with finds of a similar nature made at Perati on the east coast of Attica.

On the other hand we have an important group of Philistine tombs at Tell Fara, originally excavated by Petrie in 1928–29, whose architectural features have now been critically examined by Waldbaum.[15] These five tombs had been dug into the hard marl strata below the surface of the plain to the west of the city mound. The tombs, which unlike most Cretan sepulchres were not lined with masonry, consisted of a large rectangular or trapezoidal chamber approached by a steep, stepped passage, which was both long and narrow. The doorway was closed by a stone slab, and the chamber lay a step below the doorway. Rock benches were cut into the sides of the chamber round two, or more usually three, sides of it, and two out of the five tombs had smaller additional chambers at the rear. Most of the burials were laid out on the benches, lying on their backs in an extended position. Multiple inhumations were practised, and the residues of old burials were apparently swept to one side or into the rear chamber to make room for the latest occupants. As Waldbaum claims, the only possible Late Bronze Age parallel for the funerary architecture and customs of the Philistines at Tell Fara is provided by the burial practices of Mycenaean Greece and its Aegean colonies.

However, equally interesting for our purpose is the survey of a further five Late Bronze Age tombs, also at Tell Fara, which were originally mentioned by Petrie. These tombs correspond closely to the Philistine sepulchres in almost every detail listed above, and Waldbaum claims a common foreign prototype for both series of tombs. In this case the tombs have been excavated into the side of a Hyksos fosse to the west of the city mound, and they contained imported Mycenaean pottery and a little imitation Mycenaean ware of local fabrication. The former was classified as a simple version of Late Levanto-Mycenaean IIIb ware, but the locally fabricated pottery was *not* the typical Philistine ware. There was otherwise some overlapping of pottery styles between the two cemeteries, so that it was possible to date them. The second group of tombs is assigned to a slightly earlier period than the first group: say, 1250–1150 B.C. for the former, and mid-twelfth century to early tenth century B.C. for the latter. This conclusion is very interesting as it appears that the earlier burials belong to a small settlement of "The Peoples of the Sea", possibly mercenaries, who had come to Tell Fara during the period when Mycenaean power was infiltrating into Asia Minor after the fall of Troy. Possibly they were remnants of the wave of invaders whose attack on Egypt was driven back *c* 1221 B.C. The later tombs definitely belong to the Philistines who seized power in this area following the repulse of the second invasion *c* 1192 B.C. by Ramesses III, the Grecian elements, whether of Mycenaean, Dorian or Cretan origin, uniting for this purpose.

These dry-as-dust details of sepulchres and their furnishings are necessary to permit us to identify the people who used them, and the date at which they lived. In contrast there is a more vivid, human story in the Bible, (Judges 16: 29, 30) which tells of the manner in which Samson met his end, and which also turns on details of Mycenaean architecture:

> "And Samson took hold of the two middle pillars upon which the house stood, and on which it was borne up, of the one with his right hand, and of the other with his left. And Samson said, let me die with the Philistines. And he bowed himself with all his might; and the house fell upon the lords, and upon all the people that were therein."

It has been pointed out that this seemingly incredible feat was indeed feasible if the Great House of the Philistines was constructed in accordance with the method used by the Mycenaeans for supporting the upper storeys above the main assembly hall by wooden pillars, which with the passage of time could be seriously weakened by dry rot.

This Philistine hegemony was to last for about two hundred years, and the combination of the Greek fighting spirit with the Mycenaean chariot, brazen armour, and the iron weapons derived from the Hittites was to prove too strong for the Israelites of that period. All this evidence is consistent with the theory that the Dorians were the main element of "The Peoples of the Sea" who drove right down the coasts of Asia Minor to the Egyptian border *c* 1192 B.C. The Philistine graves testify, by the presence of iron objects, that it was during this period that they acquired the secret of manufacturing iron from the Hittites on their way south; so that it was the Philistines who introduced iron into Palestine, and the Dorians returning to Greece who brought it to the Greek mainland.

The Phrygians had seized and held the "Land of Hatti", and the Hittites themselves had been displaced southwards and split up into a number of loosely-associated Neo-Hittite kingdoms such as Arpad and Carchemish. Of the other invading nations, there is no trace of their part in the affair, excepting the Peleset. At Troy itself, in the authoritative view of Blegen,[16] the invaders who *ultimately* took over Troy VIIb2 introduced a new cultural background at a lower level of sophistication. This was characterized by the appearance of a new type of pottery, the so-called Buckelkeramik or Knobbed Ware. This pottery was an almost backward primitive type, made of a black polished clay in shapes which were highly distinctive and quite different from those prevailing in the previous period. The most remarkable feature was that the pots were handmade, and that they appear side by side with the more sophisticated Grey Minyan and Tan Wares, made on the potter's wheel, which were characteristic of the earlier levels at Troy before the arrival of the invaders. These Knobbed Ware folk are believed to have come from Thrace, and they brought with them other minor artifacts, such as new types of bronze tools, and a distinctive type of architecture marked by the setting of rough orthostats along the lower edges of the walls. This rude culture does not appear to have infiltrated further into Asia Minor, nor can any signs of these people be found on the mainland across the Aegean.

It is evident that the new Knobbed Ware folk settled down side by side with the previous inhabitants of the city, and apparently were ultimately absorbed by them. We can deduce this because we find that, after the troubles of the Dark Ages subsided, the settlers who returned in the seventh century B.C. to occupy the site—which had meantime been devastated again and deserted towards the close of the twelfth century B.C.—still used the old Grey Minyan pottery, while the Knobbed Ware had been forgotten.

From this it would appear that the settlers of Troy VIIb2 were not the Dorians, as they had absorbed the Mycenaean culture according to the archaeological records from Thessaly and Macedonia, but it was rather Thracian allies of theirs with a ruder culture who settled in Troy after the Dorian invasion had passed on.

It is unlikely that the invaders of Egypt were completely destroyed and enslaved, but the plight of the survivors must have appeared serious to their leaders. They were separated from home by the hundreds of miles of hostile country they had overrun. Bitterly hostile to their return, this countryside would also have been stripped bare of food during the progress southwards so that a state of near-famine must have prevailed. Above all the defeated confederation would have expected the Egyptians to follow up their victory and pursue them northwards to re-establish Egyptian control over the debated lands they had long contested with the Hittite empire.

The defeated leaders would have seen that chaos and famine lay in front of them and retribution was on their heels. So it was only natural to look for an easier way home, and for a means of making good, at least partially, the plunder lost to the Egyptians. For this purpose the ships which had survived the naval battle, and others which may have remained in their home ports in Rhodes and the other islands, as well as those coastal areas controlled by the invaders, would have offered a natural solution. Such ships, either originally owned by the invaders, seized in their home ports during the triumphant surge southwards, hired for the purpose with captured booty or just persuaded to join as allies in a large-scale piratical raid, provided the easiest means of return. There was the added advantage that Crete and the Greek mainland could be invaded en route and perhaps overrun completely. These were the next wealthiest prizes after Egypt in the Ancient World. The captains and seamen of this evacuation fleet would have needed little persuasion—the Carian pirates were notorious—and the mainland of Asia Minor must have appeared a place from which it was prudent to absent themselves. Egyptian reprisals and oppressions in Syria and Palestine on such occasions were historically notorious, and as the balance of power had been destroyed by the fall of the Hittite empire it must have appeared likely to the Dorian leaders that the Egyptians would press into Syria and even beyond.

The natural route home in this disengaging operation would have been via Rhodes and then by the island chain on to the Greek mainland. There is evidence to support this theory, which is further developed in Chapter 4 dealing with the invasion of the Greek mainland and in Chapter 5 dealing with the Cretan aspects. Crete could, of course, have been by-passed and the attack made directly on the mainland. However, it would seem logical to take Crete first and use it as a rallying point and invasion base for the attack on Pylos.

Finally it is rewarding to see if there is any historical parallel to support the theory that a body of men could still have held together and retained a strong central leadership capable of snatching victory from defeat by overrunning Knossos and Pylos. A striking parallel is found in the march of the "Ten Thousand", so vividly described by Xenophon. Here the Greeks won a decisive initial victory over the left wing of the Persian army at Cunaxa, just as the northern invaders initially overwhelmed the Hittite empire and the kingdoms bordering the eastern Mediterranean. However, the allies of the Greeks, the Persians under Cyrus who had revolted, were defeated in the centre at Cunaxa, as the northern invaders were defeated by the Egyptians. If we accept the speculation that the allies of the "Dorians" were defeated as the advance guard, the parallel becomes closer, though it still holds good more remotely even if the "Dorians" were involved in the main battle with the Egyptians and succeeded in disengaging themselves as their descendants did at Cunaxa. We do not know whether the "Dorians" lost their leaders against Egypt, but even if they did the situation would be matched by the events at Cunaxa and later, when first of all the "Ten Thousand" lost their political leader Cyrus in the battle, and then their military leaders by treachery. None the less they kept a strong central leadership and in the words of Hammond:[17]

> ". . . the Greeks found themselves alone in the heart of a hostile empire. In open warfare too they proved their superiority over the troops of the East; for despite the treacherous seizure of their commanders they fought their way out through Jekireh, Kurdistan, and Armenia to the plain of Erzerum, where the deep snow diverted them towards the Black Sea."

Xenephon records that on reaching the sea at Trapezos the one aim of the Greek army was to proceed home by sea instead of attempting to fight their way back through further hostile territory. The heartfelt cry of "*Thalassa, thalassa*" ("the sea, the sea") is significant of their preference. The historical record of their behaviour and reactions surely gives strong support to the probability that the "Dorians" held together, fought their way out and when possible chose to return home by sea. For these men were the ancestors of the Greeks at Cunaxa, and the ships in their case were ready to hand for the evacuation.

To return to the Phrygian invaders who inherited the kingdom of Hatti, it is interesting to look for any scientific evidence linking them with the people who overran the Hittite kingdom *c* 1200 B.C., according to the archaeological demonstration that the Hittite records cease about that date. A number of C-14 datings are available for carbonaceous samples recovered from excavations carried out under the auspices of the University Museum, Philadelphia, at Yassihüyük-Gordian, the site of the capital of the Phrygian empire. These tests have been reported by Kohler and Ralph.[18]

The oldest sample taken from the "Phrygian IVa" level on the City Mound shows a date of 1280 B.C. plus or minus 130 years. This date corresponds very well with the date of the great invasions about 1200 B.C., taking into account that the sample was from a beam. The date of the building could therefore possibly be as much as a hundred years later than the date determined for the sample, which, of course, gives the date of the tree from which the beam was taken. Therefore the date of this level of Phrygian settlement indicates that Phrygian occupation followed immediately after the fall of Hatti. There is no need to postulate that some other people was responsible for it.

Referring to tombs rather than settlements, these experts also report significantly that: "Several samples from Gordian showed unexpectedly old dates", although this is attributed to the fact that samples came from beams which had been "squared", so that the outer growth-rings of wood had been removed. However, a *maximum* correction of a hundred years for this factor would appear adequate for these samples, taken from Phrygian tombs, for which dates of 1099 B.C. plus or minus 127 years, 1053 B.C. plus or minus 84 years, 910 B.C. plus or minus 41 years and 1087 B.C. plus or minus 34 years were found.

It therefore also appears possible to link these tombs with the invaders responsible for the fall of Hatti, although the dates attributed to these tombs by the excavators, based on archaeological evidence, were some three or four hundred years later than those given by C-14 dating. This discrepancy could be explained either by the use of beams for the tombs being taken from derelict houses in the settlement, or to a consistent tendency by the archaeologist to under-estimate the date of Phrygian occupation, or to a combination of both these factors.

Some support for the view that the Phrygian occupation followed closely on the fall of Hatti can also be found in the archaeological results of the "1963 Campaign at Gordian" reported by Rodney S. Young.[19] The excavators found a primitive wall of yellow sandstone. At its base the pottery was chiefly Hittite, but mixed with it were always a few sherds of grey and black Phrygian wares. From this association the conclusion can be drawn that the wall can be dated to the earliest Phrygian times. The wall had an interior filling of clay and stone, and its great thickness, 2.65 metres, suggests that it was a fortification wall. Young suggests that:

> "Perhaps it was the first defensive wall of the Phrygian settlement put up when the new settlers arrived at the Gordian site in the 10th century *or even earlier*." (The italics are mine.)

After all, the earliest tombs may not yet have been located and also we would have to expect that some time would elapse, after the initial conquest, before the new arrivals could consolidate their position and start the construction of tombs on an extensive scale. The time interval indicated by C-14 dating corresponds with a similar interval noted between conquest and the appearance of new large-scale burials in some of the areas of the conquered Mycenaean kingdoms in the Peloponnese, and may be attributed to the same causes: the ravages of plague and the need for subsequent consolidation. Further data must be awaited, but meantime there is at least a slender thread of evidence to show that the Phrygians were the people responsible for the downfall of the Hittite empire.

REFERENCES

[1] Gurney, O. R., *The Hittites,* Pelican Books, 1961, pp. 46–58.
[2] Hammond, N. G. L., *A History of Greece to 322 B.C.,* 1959, p. 73f.
[3] Herodotus, *The Histories,* Penguin Books, 1963, p. 15f.
[4] Desborough, V. R. d'A., *The Last Mycenaeans and Their Successors,* 1964, pp. 158–63.
[5] Woolley, L., *A Forgotten Kingdom,* Pelican Books, 1953, p. 171.
[6] Gurney, O. R., *ibid,* p. 51.
[7] Gurney, O. R., *ibid,* p. 36.
[8] Seton Lloyd, *Early Anatolia,* Pelican Books, 1956, p. 71f.
[9] Gurney, O. R., *ibid,* p. 39.
[10] Seton Lloyd, *ibid,* p. 191.
[11] Gurney, O. R., *ibid,* p. 39f.
[12] Steiner, G., *Neue Alasija Texte,* Kadmos, 1962, p. 130.
[13] Gurney, O. R., *ibid,* p. 35.
[14] Dothan, Trude, American Journal of Archaeology, 70, 1966, p. 187.
[15] Waldbaum, Jane C., American Journal of Archaeology, 70, 1966, p. 331f.
[16] Blegen, C. W., The Cambridge Ancient History, Fascicle *Troy,* 1961, p. 14f.
[17] Hammond, N. G. L., *ibid,* p. 451.
[18] Kohler, E. L. and Ralph, E. K., American Journal of Archaeology, 65, pp. 360–3.
[19] Young, R. S., American Journal of Archaeology, 68, p. 292f.

CHAPTER FOUR

Pylos: The Vital Blow

A plague o' both your houses!

SHAKESPEARE

WE now come to the Dorian attack on the Greek mainland, leaving for the moment Crete's possible role as an invasion base. The only *written* historical evidence is recorded in the Linear B tablets unearthed by Blegen at Pylos. Their contents have been vividly reported and analyzed by Palmer and as a result it is clear that the attack on Pylos was definitely expected from the sea,[1] and not overland from the north or north-east. Moreover, both Greek tradition and the archaeological evidence show that Athens, and the Mycenaean kingdom based on it, held fast and successfully resisted the invaders. This leads to the obvious question: "From which direction could the sea-borne invasion of Pylos have been expected?" Only three directions merit serious consideration: from the north-west, down the coasts of Elis, from the north-east, the direction of the Aegean, or from the south.

If the traditional interpretation of a Dorian invasion direct from the north is to be accepted, then either of the first two possibilities could apply. But the only one of these which would be logical is that down the west coast of the Peloponnesian peninsula, presumably originating[2] in the Gulf of Corinth, or, for the north-eastern Greek allies, from the coasts of Aetolia. Strategically it is most unlikely that the Dorian fleet could have concentrated in the western Aegean basin and then by-passed the powerful kingdoms of Athens, Tiryns and Mycenae in order to attack Pylos first. Such an indirect course would have exposed their lines of communication and retreat to attack by the Mycenaean naval power, so that it can be ruled out straight away.

The second possibility is a sea-borne attack from the Gulf of Corinth and the Aetolian coasts down the western shores of the Peloponnesian peninsula. Since the powerful Mycenaean confederation possessed centres of naval strength in Mycenae (whose influence extended to the shores of the Gulf of Corinth), Pylos and the Ionian islands, it is incredible that they would have permitted the concentration in the Gulf of Corinth of a Dorian fleet strong enough to attack and destroy the kingdom of Pylos. Mycenaean sea-power there was necessary to handle the trade with Italy and Sicily, where Mycenaean settlements are known to have existed at that time,[3] and to keep open the Adriatic trade-routes northwards. There were settlements at Old Corinth and Korakou, while on the north-west area bordering the Gulf of Corinth there was an important fortification at Krisa,[4] in the plain below Delphi, destroyed at the end of LH IIIb (*c* 1200 B.C.). In these circumstances a concentration of Dorian ships would hardly have been possible.

The disposition of forces, and of refugee women and children, as detailed in the Pylian tablets, does not suggest that the attack from the sea was expected down the west coast. Land and sea forces would surely have been concentrated there, while the refugees would have been gathered together at Leuktron or near the eastern frontier so that they could escape overland to the east if necessary. On the other hand, the tablets Palmer analyzed[5] describe the forces as spread out both to the east and west of Cape Akritas, with the refugees mainly at Pylos and Leuktron. This suggests that the sea-borne attack was expected from the south. It would not be known whether the blow would fall east or west of the cape; the refugees at Pylos and Leuktron could have escaped inland and eastwards respectively if necessary.

We may conclude that the invasion was indeed from the south. The only *recorded* historical evidence therefore fits in with the first theory advanced in Chapter 3, that the initial and vital blow came from Asia Minor via Crete and the chain of islands, starting with Rhodes, which link it with the eastern Mediterranean shores. The probability that Crete was also attacked is discussed in Chapter 5.

We may even ignore for the moment the Linear B tablets, and consider again the traditional interpretation that the first attack came overland from the north. We must conclude that the strategy called for by such a route would be most unlikely for an attack on the *unbroken* Mycenaean power. It is clear from the grave stele at Mycenae, the "chariot tablets" recovered at Knossos, and the epic tradition of the

Iliad that these Achaean kingdoms were ruled by a warlike aristocracy whose power was based on the use of the chariot. To attack them from the north or north-east would have involved travelling over mountain tracks without heavy baggage or chariot support; whilst the Achaeans would have had ample warning of the Dorian advent, and could have concentrated their forces and chariots accordingly. This is not the picture presented by the Pylian tablets[6] which indicate expectation of an attack from the sea and the inability to predict where the attack would fall, judging by the widespread distribution of the naval forces and "coast watchers".

All these arguments would apply with still greater force if the invasion route for the attack on Pylos had been *overland* from the north-east via the north coast of the Gulf of Corinth. This traditional route is described by Hammond:[7]

> "Twenty years later (*c* 1120) the Dorians, led by Heracleidae, migrated from Dryopis, a district of Doris, and reached the north shore of the Gulf of Corinth. Crossing thence by ship, they launched an attack on the Aeolic-speaking people of Corinthia and forced their way into the Peloponnese. The Dorians acted in collusion with invaders further West, who crossed from Aetolia to gain a footing in the Peloponnese. After their initial success the two groups followed separate routes, the Dorians invading the eastern and the others the western areas of the Peloponnese. So far the tradition is precise and unanimous . . ."

Strategically this would have involved either by-passing Mycenae, Tiryns, and the Argolid, and leaving their communications and possible retreat route to be cut at will by the forces of these kingdoms, or overwhelming these powerful centres before attacking Pylos. They would hardly have been allowed free passage over these territories. From the time of the *Iliad* to the All-Cretan league in the Classical Age the Greeks were capable of uniting when attacked, however great their inter-city struggles and rivalries. Moreover, the dates do not fit. The fall of Pylos is placed by Blegen at *c* 1200 B.C., while the traditional date of the overland Dorian invasion is given as *c* 1120 B.C., and it is indeed generally recognized that Pylos fell before Mycenae. Finally the philological evidence does not support the tradition of an invasion by this route. This is discussed further in Chapter 8.

There remains the possibility of invasion from the south, directly or via Crete. Pendlebury's remarks in another context are relevant here:[8]

> "Probably there was emigration from Egypt, which was easier than it appears, because there is a steady sea-current from the Delta along the coasts of Syria and Asia Minor, and thence past Crete into the Aegean and the West. Under the steep coasts there is also a daily land breeze and sea breeze, which makes coastwise navigation easy . . ."

This passage refers to the Egyptian influence on the first major upsurge of the Cretan culture *c* 3000 B.C. when sea transport was even more primitive. The physical facts are as true for the withdrawal of a Dorian "Ten Thousand" stranded in Asia Minor, or Palestine, Syria and Rhodes. Any modern traveller taking the weekly steamer from Rhodes to the ports of Sitia and Aghia Nicolaos will endorse this. Even for a large part of the winter months this route is possible and even easy for small ships, while the island chain, Rhodes, Carpathos and Casos, forms the stepping stones.

In the *Iliad* Rhodes is represented as a stronghold held by Tlepolemus, one of the Heracleidae, and the island would also have been ideal for regrouping the Dorian forces, safe from the Egyptians, before the raid on Crete and Pylos. I like to think of the ship engraved in the rock at the foot of the approach pathway to the Acropolis at Lindos (see Plate II) as being a memorial to this venture, whatever the age of the carving. Carpathos is conveniently placed midway in the sea passage from Rhodes to Crete and offers shelter for shipping (see Plate III) as a subsidiary base or as a refuge in bad weather.

The distribution of Greek dialects in classical times is significant, since the Doric dialect prevailed in Cythera, Crete, Casos, Carpathos, Rhodes and the neighbouring mainland coasts (Chapter 8).

In summary, we may conclude that this was the route of the Dorians and that their attack came from the south. Desborough[9] has, in fact, pointed out that such an attack from the south or south-west cannot be excluded, but mentions that a considerable force would have been needed, with a long voyage across open sea, and that the immunity of the islands in the Aegean, particularly the Dodecanese, would have to be explained. The first point is met by the discussion in Chapter 3 of the forces that would have been available from the conquests of "The Peoples of the Sea" including the Dorians. Against the second point can be set the evidence advanced by Pendlebury and quoted above; the third is answered by the discussion in Chapter 6 of the thesis that the Heracleidae of Rhodes joined with the Dorians in their expedition through Asia Minor to the Egyptian border. It would thus appear that a reasonable explanation can be found for each of Desborough's objections, together with other reasons given in Chapter 3.

The theory fits the historical and archaeological facts as well as the Grecian traditions better than any alternative theory. But this does not mean that the traditional route must be abandoned completely. If the *initial* attack was by sea on Pylos, a concerted attack was probably made only shortly after on the rest of the Mycenaean kingdoms in the peninsula. This could have been carried out simultaneously from the bridgehead of the conquered Pylian kingdom and by the traditional land route starting from the Dorian homeland.

A vital factor is the actual date of destruction of Pylos, which had been put at *c.* 1200 B.C. by Blegen. This date has recently been confirmed by Kohler and Ralph, who by means of C-14 dating have demonstrated the correctness of Blegen's figure which was based on the archaeological evidence. These pioneers deserve great credit for opening up this field of investigation into the dating of this period of Mycenaean history, which for some inexplicable reason has hitherto been sadly neglected. Using the figure of a 5800 year half-life for C-14, they find all the samples analyzed are placed close to or earlier than 1200 B.C., thus confirming the date estimated for the destruction of the site by Blegen and Rawson. The samples giving the earlier dates all correspond to beams, usually squared beams from which the outer layers had been removed, which had been used in the construction of the palace of Nestor. This gap in time corresponds well with its estimated date of building, and the likely age of the timber used for its construction.[10]

One awkward fact remaining is that the date of *c* 1200 B.C. for the invasion of Pylos does not agree with the *traditional* date calculated by the historians of the classical age (*c* 1120 B.C.),[11] nor does the route agree with tradition. This could be glossed over by suggesting that tradition is unreliable, and that the errors in the ancient Greek historians' methods explain the discrepancy in the dates. Fortunately we need not resort to this subterfuge. MacKendrick and others have pointed out that the Dorian invasions were a series of incursions extending over more than 100 years.[12] They involved shifts of population and a very fluid situation, and the traditions inherited by the historians of the Classical Age referred to the last stages of this period. They were familiar with the final crystallized situation.

This explanation appears logical but there is an alternative and more probable one still. This is of course that the traditional date for the Dorian invasions (*c* 1120 B.C.) can be reconciled with the date of the mainland disasters (*c* 1200 B.C.) on the basis of Blegen's date for the destruction of Troy (*c* 1250 B.C.). This is further discussed in Chapter 8.

As for the route, we do not have to accept uncritically that the tradition implies *all* the Dorians came from Doris, or more specifically from Dryopis in that region. Indeed Greek tradition links them also with Pindus, Olympus and Ossa and it is likely that Doris in the tradition is a recollection by the Athenians of the area where the Dorians were concentrated when Athens became conscious of the threat. If they came from this region, the tradition does not state that they came directly.[11]

This point can be illustrated by our own historical times if we consider the Norman invasion of A.D. 1066. Accepting for the sake of this examination that later generations had no written history for this period, nor for 500 years after it, we can reach some interesting hypothetical conclusions. The Vikings, Norsemen, Northmen or Normans were the terror of Europe and in fact the "Dorians" of their day. The parallel can be drawn further; they were also the Indo-European "wild hill cousins" of the Saxons and Danes then living in England. The decisive battle of Hastings was preceded by an invasion of other Norsemen who were thrown back at Stamford Bridge. Lacking all historical records and relying on 500 years of verbal tradition, distant generations trying to pierce the mists of antiquity would inherit the fact that Britain had been conquered by the Norsemen. Our archaeologists, after careful excavation of the traditional battle site at Stamford Bridge, would perhaps conclude that the invaders had overwhelmed Saxon England from the north-east and that the invaders' fleets had gathered in the fjords of Norway. Confusion would then arise from the excavations of Norman remains such as Battle Abbey. These would be dated to a subsequent successful invasion by the French in the time of Joan of Arc; the Anglo-French wars would have resulted in an extensive oral tradition. Perhaps archaeologists would conclude that the superior French culture from the south had influenced the barbaric English. Of course they would be quite justified in reaching such conclusions on the evidence available to them, and in fact there is an element of truth in the latter conclusion. Yet we, with the written evidence, know better. We know that the invasion of England came via Normandy and that in the few generations the Norsemen had been there they had acquired the more advanced language and culture of the French. In other words, the invasion did not come *directly* from Scandinavia and the north-east.

The parable shows the importance of the written record when available; however scanty, it illuminates oral tradition.

A piece of circumstantial evidence which needs consideration is the set of thirteen tablets from Pylos interpreted by Palmer[13] as an inventory of a royal tomb:

> "It should be said at once that this interpretation has been disputed and also that the dispute is primarily about one word. What is not in doubt or controversy is that the document is an inventory o household effects and of the greatest importance and interest to archaeologists. It begins with cooking vessels and the appurtenances of the hearth and then moves on to tables, chairs and footstools. There can be no doubt that the whole set of objects is connected with preparations for a feast. The gorgeous character of this furniture will emerge from the translation given below. From this it will be clear that no archaeological finds from Greek lands have given us any idea that furniture of this luxuriousness adorned the palaces of the Mycenaean kings. The nearest parallel is offered by the tomb of Tutankhamen."

The whole story is brilliantly presented by Palmer, and makes fascinating reading, but for our purposes it is sufficient to take note of two aspects: the interpretation of the disputed words, and the numbers of chairs and footstools in the list and their description.

The important disputed word is "da-mo-ko-ro" which Palmer interprets as the expected spelling of the well-known name Damoklos and not as a uniquely attested title. Consequently the introductory formula in the document is translated by Palmer:

"What Pu-ke-qi-ri saw when the Wanax buried Sja-ke-wa son of Damocles."

The "Wanax" is, of course, the king and Palmer makes the point that the double name is again indicative of a grandee and that this name "Sja-ke-wa son of Damocles" appears in other tablets as that of a prominent personality of the "Hither Province", who may well be the provincial governor.[14]

Secondly, the total number of chairs in the list is five, and the total number of footstools fourteen, of which four are associated with the chairs and ten are listed separately. It is interesting to recall that Palmer's tentative construction of the administrative chain of command coming under Wanax, the king, is:[15]

Chief of the Palace Bureau (Alxoitas)

The Hither Province	*The Further Province*
The Provincial Governor (Sja-ke-wa Da-mo-ko-ro)	The Provincial Governor (Te-po-se-u)
The Deputy Governor (or Duma) (Du-ni-jo du-ma)	The Deputy Governor (or Duma) (?? du-ma)
Nine Districts each with a District Officer (ko-re-ter) and an Assistant District Officer (po-ro-ko-re-ter)	Seven Districts each with a District Officer (ko-re-ter) and an Assistant District Officer (po-ro-ko-re-ter)

Thus we find a total of six high-ranking officials including the Wanax as the most senior and the two Deputy Governors as the most junior. The total of the District Officers, the next-ranking officials in the hierarchy, is sixteen. It is interesting to speculate how many people might be invited as official guests to a funeral feast for the burial of one of the high-ranking officials; though it must be stressed that this is only speculation. If we apply the normal rules of office protocol—and Palmer emphasizes that a close analysis of the archives shows "a meticulous and efficient bureaucracy"—we should expect that, as well as the king, the Chief of the Palace Bureau, the two Provincial Governors and the two Deputy Governors would qualify for invitation as the high-ranking officials, giving a total of six including the king. However, of these six it is almost certain that the Governor or Deputy Governor of the Further Province would have to remain at his post during a time of crisis. This would not have been necessary in the Hither Province where the feast was presumably held at the burial ground near the capital of that province. Accordingly, we could expect only five of the high-ranking officials to attend the funeral feast.

Of the sixteen District Officers we would expect that the two senior members of the districts in which the provincial capitals were located would have to take over temporarily the functions of the Governors and Deputy Governors, while the sixteen Assistant District Officers would take over from the District Officers during their absence. Therefore of the second line of officials we would expect fourteen to be invited. This gives a total at the feast of nineteen (5+14=19) and it is perhaps significant that the total of chairs and footstools listed in the tablets is also nineteen (5+4+10). Moreover, the division of the total is between five chairs and fourteen footstools, which is precisely what we would expect if the chairs were ceremonial chairs or thrones provided for the king and the top-ranking officials, and if footstools were provided for the lesser officials, as was indeed the custom of the eastern monarchs.

This speculation receives some support from the manner in which four of the footstools are paired up with the chairs. The logical way to make an inventory is to list all the chairs and then all the footstools separately. The pairing up seems to be deliberate so that the "right-hand man" of each official could "sit at his feet". It is also worthy of note that one pair of chair and footstool stands out from the others in its richness of decoration while the footstool is the only one described as being inlaid and adorned with gold. This can be seen from Palmer's translation:[16]

> "One chair, of crystal, inlaid with cyanus, tin (?) and gold, the back (sides?) inlaid with golden human figures and a pair of stags' (?) heads and golden bulls' heads and with golden palm trees (or palmettes) and with palm trees (or palmettes) of cyanus. One footstool, inlaid with cyanus and tin (?) and gold, with golden struts."

Possibly this was the king's throne and the footstool of his "right-hand man".

We can imagine that it was the Chief of the Palace Bureau (Alxoitas) who occupied the golden footstool on the principle that such a seat at the feet of the king ranked with a provincial throne. This solution would raise two difficulties: there would be one surplus chair and one less footstool called for than given by this analysis. The latter could be explained by assuming that one of the District Officers was not available, either because the vacancy caused by the death of the Provincial Governor of the Hither Province had been filled by a chain of promotions, so that one of the districts had a newly-promoted Assistant District Officer acting as District Officer who did not yet rank for invitation or could not be spared for lack of an experienced deputy, or because he had to assume some duty such as that of commanding the ceremonial guard. The question of the surplus chair is still more nebulous—was a vacant chair placed for the dead grandee, which would explain why in the pairing of chairs and footstools there is one less of the latter than of the former, or were both the Governor and the Deputy Governor of the Further Province present at the feast?

All this is pure speculation and it must be emphasized that it is presented as such. However, it is at least significant that the total number of seats listed checks with the number of officials who, in accordance with the organization known from other tablets, would have been expected to attend the funeral feast.

Palmer[17] strengthens his interpretation that these tablets refer to the burial of a Mycenaean lord by pointing out that the last tablet of the set lists a pair of swords and, according to his latest translation, two golden necklaces and a pair of double axes:

> "Apropos of a tomb at Knossos, the Chieftain's Grave, Sir Arthur

Evans has written (PoM, iv, 861f) that 'with the skeleton itself had been placed the relics most distinctive of his rank and military profession—his gold necklace, his long and his short sword. That gold necklaces, like the torques of Gaulish warriors, served as a sign of rank or distinction may be gathered from more than one pictorial and sculptural record.' As for the double axes, they are familiar as a religious symbol to all students of the Mycenaean-Minoan world, and it is likely that it stands for the Mother Goddess, whose cult name was Wanassa, the Queen. We may now note a curious echo. The inventory begins with libation jugs . . ."

Palmer's case for interpreting these tablets as describing the furniture for a funeral feast and a tomb inventory should be accepted in the absence of a better explanation. He concludes his survey:

"It is not known on what occasion this Mycenaean lord met his death in those final months of Pylos' existence. That the King himself officiates is significant . . ."

One is strongly tempted to speculate that he met his death in a preliminary brush with the Dorians, possibly off Crete if indeed the invaders landed there first before attacking Pylos—and it is believed that there is evidence to support this (see Chapter 5). In relation to the fall of Pylos, Palmer quotes the moving words of Homer describing such an invasion:[18]

"As when the smoke rising from a city reaches the bright sky far from an island that foemen beset, and the day long they contend in grievous strife from their city wall. At sundown the beacon fires blaze in rows and the glare reaches aloft for their neighbours to see in the hope that they will come in their ships and ward off their doom."

These words apply with still more force to the island of Crete. Is it too much to imagine that Sja-ke-wa Da-mo-ko-ro, the Provincial Governor of the Hither Province of the kingdom of Pylos, was killed in such an attempt to relieve the beleaguered city of Knossos, or at least in a reconnaissance in force, and that he was buried with full military honours, the king himself officiating? The Provincial Governor of the senior Hither Province would be the logical man to send on such an expedition, and after his death it would be necessary to bolster public morale, particularly if Knossos had already fallen. If this is so, the funeral feast would have had a double purpose as council-of-war and an introduction to the new commander-in-chief promoted to replace the dead grandee. Perhaps it was the decisions taken then which are recorded in other sets of tablets[19] skilfully interpreted by Palmer as dealing with the "Last Days of Pylos".

What happened in this region after the Mycenaean kingdoms of the Peloponnese had fallen to the concerted attack of the Dorians coming from the south and from their homeland in the north to overrun the remaining Mycenaean kingdoms? The evidence that the Dorians were also "Mycenaeans" is dealt with below (Chapter 7) and at this stage it will suffice to mention the chief support for this view; for the archaeological evidence shows that at the time of the invasion the culture of the greater part of the areas from which they came (Thessaly and Macedonia) was primarily Mycenaean.[20] It is therefore not surprising that the culture of the areas overrun by the Dorians should remain Mycenaean. This overcomes the difficulty which existed when it was assumed that the Dorians were merely northern barbarians. It reconciles this assumption with the archaeological evidence that the culture of the Peloponnese remained primarily Mycenaean[21] after the destruction of the main Mycenaean centres (*c* 1200 B.C.)[22] at the time when the Dorian invasion must have occurred. Archaeology also indicates *inter alia* that the culture of the area did not show marked evidence of the influence of a "new people" until after a subsequent destruction of Mycenae[23] (known as the "Granary" destruction) which is dated *c* 1150 B.C. or possibly even as late as *c* 1130 B.C. From this time on there is increasing evidence of the influence of a "new people" in the area.

We now come to two other puzzling features of the aftermath of the Dorian conquest: the shifts of "Mycenaean" population which occurred, and the marked depopulation which followed in most centres of settlement.[24] A drop in population is to be expected after a major war but almost complete depopulation persisting for a considerable period in areas previously richly settled is unusual. The natural outcome of such a conquest would have been for the victors to take the spoils and settle in the area, and that this did indeed happen is supported by the Greek tradition of the "return of the Heracleidae". Because the Dorians have been regarded as wild barbarians, whilst it is apparent that Mycenaean culture still persisted in the area after their invasion, the theory has been advanced that they left the area after burning and sacking the main centres, leaving a decimated remnant of Mycenaeans behind them—most of whom had fled to centres of refuge such as Achaea—to be subsequently overrun by a new people, who this time did settle, at some date after the "Granary" destruction at Mycenae. However, if we accept that the Dorians were Mycenaeans, and did not relinquish their conquest (*c* 1200 B.C.) another explanation must be found for the population shifts and depopulation. There is no reason to believe that the Dorians wiped out the existing population at the time of their conquest; the evidence is indeed to the contrary.[25] However, plague—often accompanied by famine—frequently followed war and offers the most reasonable explanation of the extensive depopulation.

An attack of plague in ancient times could have the most devastating effects—Herodotus[26] records that out of a choir of one hundred young men that the Chians sent to Delphi, ninety-eight died of plague. Thucydides' account of the plague which attacked Athens in 430 B.C. during the Peloponnesian War is of the greatest interest as he spoke from personal knowledge, having himself recovered from it. His account[27] in part includes the following observations:

> ". . . the violence of the calamity was such that men, not knowing where to turn, grew reckless of all law, human and divine. The customs which had hitherto been observed at funerals were universally violated, and they buried their dead each one as best he could. Many, having no proper appliances because the deaths in their household had been so numerous already, lost all shame in the burial of the dead. When one man had raised a funeral pile, others would come, and throwing on their dead first, set fire to it; or when some other corpse was already burning, before they could be stopped, would throw their own dead upon it and depart."

Thucydides goes on to add an interesting aside:

> "In their troubles they naturally called to mind a verse which the elder men among them declared to have been current long ago: 'A Dorian War will come and a plague with it'."

and adds the following apt comment:

> "There was a dispute about the precise expression; some saying that limos, a famine, and not loimos, a plague, was the original word. Nevertheless, as might have been expected, for men's memories reflected their sufferings, the argument in favour of loimos prevailed at the time. But if ever in future years another Dorian War arises accompanied by a famine, they will probably repeat the verse in the other form."

Prophecy is sometimes past history refurbished, and indeed here it looks as though we may be dealing with a traditional memory of a plague following the Dorian invasion of *c* 1192 B.C. Such an explanation would clarify the other puzzling features: the population shifts and the changes in burial habits.

The chamber tomb was characteristic of the Mycenaean culture. It was normally cut into the side of a hill, or into sloping ground, and consisted of a burial chamber, which was usually rectangular in shape, connected with the entrance by a narrow passageway or dromos. The tholos tomb was a circular chamber, like the old-fashioned bee-hive, built of stone. In both the normal method of burial was similar, the dead being laid out in ceremonial style on the floor of the chamber together with grave furniture, which was sometimes of extreme richness and beauty. The tholos tombs were far superior in construction and furnishing to the chamber tombs, and were apparently reserved for the burial of the dead of royal or noble families. In these tombs multiple burials were normally employed, the tombs being used in effect as family or tribal crypts. Away from the homeland the Mycenaeans used a different method of burial—that of cremation—which was apparently accepted as appropriate when the corpse could not be laid with its ancestors. These cremations and burials were accompanied by elaborate rites and games in honour of the dead, judging by the description of the burial of Patroclus so vividly outlined by Homer, and by the pictorial evidence of the late Minoan III sarcophagus found at Hagia Triada which depicts elaborate sacrifices and libations performed at the entrance to the tomb.

The tholos and chamber tombs were clearly the products of a prosperous and sophisticated period, when the Mycenaean culture was at its peak. However, before that time, in the Middle Helladic period, and again after it when the Mycenaean power had been broken, we find a simpler type of burial: the cist and pit graves. The cist tomb was a slab-framed and covered grave, and the pit grave, as its name indicates, was simple and similar in shape to the cist tomb but without its slab lining and covering. These graves were normally used for single or double burials, and multiple inhumation did not occur.

As appears from Thucydides' account of the disaster of 430 B.C. a serious outbreak of plague is sometimes localized, leaving neighbouring districts relatively free. The outbreaks, and their severity, were more likely to be concentrated in areas which had been devastated by war, and could even lead to complete abandonment of sites. The natural method of disposal of plague victims is by burning, as the physical condition of the corpses would not allow the normal Mycenaean method of multiple inhumations in chamber or tholos tombs. This would make for a natural break in burial customs, and could naturally lead in time to the adoption of cist and pit graves as more hygienic after the plague when more settled methods of burial were again possible. The Dorian branch of the Mycenaeans, who had conquered the Peloponnese, would know these methods from their northern contacts with their homeland in Thessaly and Macedonia. The origins of these are northern[28] and they were still employed by their friends and allies there. This would explain the abandonment of settlements, wiped out by plague, and the shifts of population to areas such as Achaea and Kephallenia, which are reported to have *increased* in population then.[29] I would infer they escaped the worst of the outbreak. This would explain the continued widespread use of chamber tombs in these areas in the century after the disasters of *c* 1200 B.C. (i.e. the LH IIIc period). The variation[30] of a cave-like chamber tomb containing a number of pits for corpses also becomes logical. Even in badly-stricken areas chamber tombs persisted through this period;[31] but burials were not on the same scale owing to the depopulation and disruption of burial habits, but no doubt were still undertaken by the more pious.

This depopulation of the Peloponnese was possibly not quite as complete as might appear from the remains of the tombs and settlements. It is likely that the farms and agricultural areas remained settled, much in the Spartans' (Lacedaemonians') agrarian way of living in organized villages as described by Thucydides[32] rather than large settlements, so that little evidence would have survived. There is some support for this since Athens' special defence measures, reported by Broneer, were evidently relaxed quickly, as the emergency water supplies were abandoned, though people continued to live on the Acropolis, indicating no great feeling of security.[33] This suggests Dorian power had been weakened by plague, but that they continued to occupy the kingdoms they had seized. It does not suggest that the invaders left the area after looting and burning, as in that case the Attic Mycenaeans would surely have reoccupied a major part of the abandoned areas instead of utilizing the increase of refugees for the foundation of the Ionic colonies.

This leads us to the conclusion that after the invasion of *c* 1200 B.C. and the destruction of the main Mycenaean centres in the Peloponnese, Athens and the areas seized by the Dorians remained on hostile terms. This view is supported by the direction of the population shifts: particularly towards Achaea and Kephallenia in the Peloponnese; and to the east coast, notably Perati, in the case of Attica. These shifts were not only away from the devastated and plague-stricken area but also from the common frontiers and the areas which could readily be raided from the sea by the two opposing factions. Each of the new population centres was directed towards the internal communications with the remaining spheres of influence, towards Delphi and the route through Boeotia to the homeland of Thessaly and Macedonia for the Dorians; and towards the Aegean basin for Athens. Achaea was also probably dominated by the Dorians, rather than being a centre of resistance against them, because there is some archaeological evidence that this area was in contact with Delphi and Thessaly,[34] typical Achaean pottery having been found along the route northwards at Itea, probably at Delphi and at Pteleon in the southernmost coastal area of Thessaly.

After this period, starting at about the time of the "Granary" destruction at Mycenae (*c* 1150 B.C. or later), there is evidence of a new intrusive population whose culture was simpler and relatively barbaric and who used cist or pit burials.[35] The first slender evidence starts in the sub-Mycenaean period (*c* 1125–1075 B.C.) and becomes really marked from the Proto-geometric period onward,[36] with indications of a northern origin. One very puzzling feature of this period of change is the appearance of this influence in western Attica, apparently before the Argolid was affected. In Athens itself the sub-Mycenaean cemetery of the Kerameikos, although primarily Mycenaean in character, shows[37] signs of northern influence including a higher proportion of the northern ("Alpine") type of skull. At first sight this seems to be at variance with the archaeological evidence and tradition that Athens "held out" against the Dorian invaders, because it shows an unbroken culture from the Mycenaean period with no signs of destruction. Three events occurred around this time: the third or "Granary" destruction of Mycenae (*c* 1150 or later), the destruction of the Mycenaean palace at Iolkos (*c* 1150 or possibly a little earlier) and the Dorian invasion of Crete (*c* 1150, see Chapter 8). Evidence is slight, but I believe it is possible that the manpower losses from war and plague must have weakened the hold of the Mycenaean ruling element of the Dorian conquerors (see Chapter 8) and led to increasing "drafts" of the "northern" type people into the area, either from the Dorian homeland or from that of its neighbours. At the same time the "disasters" must have led to a weakening of the centralized Dorian control, with the various kingdoms becoming independent.

If this is so, we could expect the ruling power of the northern element to displace in many cases the ruling Mycenaean hierarchy (conveniently referred to as the Heracleidae). We thus have a reasonable explanation of the increasing proportion of northern people. Finally the struggle for power between the Heracleidae and the northern elements within the Dorian people could have led to open conflict: this would explain the third destruction at Mycenae and the destruction of the palace at Iolkos. Whether the Dorian occupation of Crete, or at least its central plains, is connected with this increase in northern influence is debatable. The same holds true whether it was cause or effect—the former due to the weakening of control by the Heracleidae as a result of the despatch of the expedition, and the latter as a result of the wish to escape the mainland chaos for the relative security of an island. This would also offer a possible explanation of the cemetery at

Athens, and of the evidence of the Mycenaean migrations around this time to Cyprus (appearance of intrusive pottery resembling that of the "Granary" class of the Argolid).[38] This phase would have marked the close of the Greek "Wars of the Roses" with the Attic Mycenaeans united with the further waves of Mycenaean refugees from the kingdoms overrun by the Dorians, including both the Heracleidae ruling element and the remnant of the earlier Mycenaeans who had not fled from the invasions of *c* 1200 B.C. We do not have to contemplate a complete elimination of the Mycenaean elements from the Dorian areas, but rather a shift in the balance between the Mycenaean and northern elements with the latter now predominating.

Against this background that the Dorians were Mycenaeans, and not just a barbaric horde, it is much easier to understand the fact that the renaissance was not confined to Athens. When the Dark Ages drew to a close, and the cultural and political revival which followed them gathered momentum, Corinth, Sparta, Crete, Rhodes and Thessaly all played their part in it, even in the early stages. Their contribution tends to be forgotten because it was ultimately overshadowed by the outstanding part played by Athens in the Golden Age which followed. This is not what could have been expected if these areas had been overrun by barbarians.

With the Mycenaeans who now fled to their Attic kinsmen would have gone much technical skill—e.g. the manufacture of pottery at Mycenae—and also the elements of the ruder intrusive culture they had absorbed. Presumably the Athenians would have welcomed the refugees, as allies against the now common enemy of the northern element, and the establishment of a "refugee camp", for which the Athens cemetery can be regarded as evidence, would have been logical; these Mycenaean refugees would have had no chamber tombs of their own, and little wealth for them, so that the ultimate adoption by the "new" element of cist or pit graves which they had learnt from their "northern" henchmen would have seemed in time better than the cremation they may have used initially.

Archaeological evidence does not support the customary view that intruders burst into northern Greece from the Danube basin and elsewhere and displaced the inhabitants southwards so that peoples in Macedonia were displaced into Thessaly, from Thessaly into Boeotia and so on south until the Peloponnese itself was overrun by the Dorians. The actual evidence from Macedonia, in particular from the valley of the river Axios which would have been one of the main invasion routes, shows that no large-scale invasion from the north occurred during or immediately before the period of the Dorian invasions. Specifically the evidence from the excavations of the site at Vardaroftsa is remarkable.[39] It shows continuous Mycenaean influence from the LH IIIb period right through the LH IIIc period (1230–1075 B.C.). The burnt strata, indicating the invasion period, come at a depth of 4½ to 5 metres with an approximate dating to the Proto-geometric period. As Desborough puts it: "The excavators could even be right in assigning the invasion to about the middle of the eleventh century."

This evidence simply does not fit with the view that a northern invasion set off a chain reaction southward. This idea seems to be traceable to the opening paragraphs of Thucydides' "Peloponnesian War" where he states[40] that the earlier inhabitants of Hellas:

> ". . . were migratory, and readily left their homes whenever they were overpowered by numbers. They were always ready to migrate; so that they had neither great cities nor any considerable resources . . . The richest districts were most constantly changing their inhabitants; for example, the countries which are now called Thessaly and Boeotia, the greater part of the Peloponnesus, with the exception of Arcadia . . ."

He then refers to the increase in sea communications in the time of Minos and of the growth of wealth and power during and following the Trojan War. So his reference to early migrations is probably to a time before the Trojan War. He points out that:

> "when Hellen and his sons became powerful in Phthiotis, their aid was invoked by other cities . . ."

Of course, when the Greeks spoke of "the sons of Hellen" (or of Hercules or another) they did not intend to be taken literally, and in many cases the expression was used much as we, in more recent times, would refer to the "House of Lancaster" or to "Clan MacLeod". Therefore, we have to picture the leaders of the Dorians at this time, whether Heraclids or others, as powerful barons ruling the northern marches of the Mycenaean empire, just as in our own historical times the noble families of Percy and Douglas dominated the border regions to the north of England, and exerted considerable power in their respective kingdoms. The rich plains and pastoral areas of Thessaly and Macedonia, just as in the later period of Philip and Alexander the Great, provided an ample reservoir of sturdy and warlike people to further the plans of their leaders. Thus, as Thucydides records, Hellen was in a position to furnish manpower for military adventures, and presumably his ancestors or predecessors were similarly placed. This offers a simple explanation of the reported presence of Dorians in eastern Crete, before the Trojan War, and of the number of royal houses set up within the Mycenaean empire whose founders came from Thessaly (see Chapter 9). It was inevitable that the High King should suitably reward the aid furnished by his powerful northern neighbours, whether ally or nominal vassal, to the central Mycenaean power.

This record of Thucydides certainly cannot be reconciled with a southern displacement of the Dorians because they were weak. It does not make sense to postulate that the Dorians were strong enough to conquer the powerful Mycenaean empire, but at the same time so weak that they were driven out by northern barbarians. This is not supported by the general experience that an invader penetrates until he meets a people strong enough to resist him. However, the archaeological evidence from the Axios valley *is* consistent with the Mycenaean affiliations of the Dorians and with their strength in this area which enabled them to mount the Dorian invasions from there.

REFERENCES

[1] Palmer, L. R., *Mycenaeans and Minoans,* 1961, p. 132f.

[2] Hammond, N. G. L., *A History of Greece to 322 B.C.,* 1959, p. 75.

[3] Desborough, V. R. d'A., *The Last Mycenaeans and Their Successors,* 1964, p. 215f.

[4] Desborough, V. R. d'A., *ibid,* p. 125.

[5] Palmer, L. R., *ibid,* p. 154.

[6] Palmer, L. R., *ibid,* chapter 5.

[7] Hammond, N. G. L., *ibid,* p. 75.

[8] Pendlebury, J. D. S., *A Handbook to the Palace of Minos, Knossos,* 1954, p. 16.

[9] Desborough, V. R. d'A., *ibid,* p. 223.

[10] Kohler, Ellen L. and Ralph, Elizabeth K., American Journal of Archaeology, 65, p. 366f.

[11] Hammond, N. G. L., *ibid*, p. 75.

[12] MacKendrick, P., *The Greek Stones Speak*, 1962, p. 124f.

[13] Palmer, L. R., *ibid*, p. 149f.

[14] Palmer, L. R., *ibid*, p. 100.

[15] Palmer, L. R., *ibid*, p. 101f.

[16] Palmer, L. R., *ibid*, p. 152.

[17] Palmer, L. R., *ibid*, p. 153.

[18] Palmer, L. R., *ibid*, p. 143.

[19] Palmer, L. R., *ibid*, p. 132.

[20] Desborough, V. R. d'A., *ibid*, pp. 135 and 141.

[21] Desborough, V. R. d'A., *ibid*, pp. 73–97 and 225.

[22] Desborough, V. R. d'A., *ibid*, p. 221.

[23] Desborough, V. R. d'A., *ibid*, pp. 230f and 241.

[24] Desborough, V. R. d'A., *ibid*, pp. 101f and 224f.

[25] Hammond, N. G. L., *ibid*, p. 81.

[26] Herodotus, *The Histories*, Penguin Classics, 1963, Book VI, p. 368.

[27] Thucydides, *The Peloponnesian War*, Bantam Classic, 1960, Book II, p. 124f.

[28] Desborough, V. R. d'A., *ibid*, pp. 37f and 71.

[29] Desborough, V. R. d'A., *ibid*, pp. 35, 98, 100 and 107.

[30] Desborough, V. R. d'A., *ibid*, p. 104.

[31] Desborough, V. R. d'A., *ibid*, p. 36.

[32] Thucydides, *ibid*, Book I, p. 27f.

[33] Desborough, V. R. d'A., *ibid*, p. 113.

[34] Desborough, V. R. d'A., *ibid*, p. 227.

[35] Desborough, V. R. d'A., *ibid*, p. 234.

[36] Desborough, V. R. d'A., *ibid*, p. 231f.

[37] Desborough, V. R. d'A., *ibid*, p. 116; MacKendrick, P., *ibid*, p. 125f.

[38] Desborough, V. R. d'A., *ibid*, p. 236.

[39] Desborough, V. R. d'A., *ibid*, p. 141f.

[40] Thucydides, *ibid*, Book I, p. 23f.

CHAPTER FIVE

The Cretan Picture

There is a tide in the affairs of men,
Which taken at the flood, leads on to fortune.

SHAKESPEARE

THE presence of Dorians in Crete before the thirteenth century B.C. will be discussed in Chapter 8. But before dealing with their invasion of Crete, it is necessary to review the previous Mycenaean relationships with the island.

Most modern authorities agree that about 1450 B.C. the Mycenaeans invaded Crete and that some great catastrophe overtook the island and destroyed all the main settlements as well as Knossos. As Hutchinson[1] states:

> "The same destruction (followed, accompanied, or preceded by looting) seems to have affected Phaistos and Hagia Triada in the Mesara, Tylisos, Amnisos, Nirou Khani, Mallia, Pseira, Gournia, and Mochlos in the north, and in the east, though to perhaps a lesser degree, Palaikastro and Zakros."

It seems to have been the consequence of earthquakes and floods. Marinatos has suggested a terrific eruption which blew up the island of Thera (now known as Santorin)—then the largest of the Cycladic islands—submerging a large part of the island and leaving in its place three smaller islands, Thera, Therasia and Aspronisi. He points out that the resulting crater measured 83 square kilometres with a depth of about 600 metres. It would therefore have exceeded the crater (area about 23 square kilometres) from the explosion of Krakatoa in A.D. 1883 by more than three times. The devastation of the earthquake and tidal waves in Crete must indeed have been terrifying.

Marinatos dated this eruption *c* 1500 B.C., but Hutchinson[2] prefers *c* 1400 B.C.:

"I should prefer to have dated this eruption of Thera about 1400 B.C. (though there may of course have been two serious outbreaks of the volcano) . . . Otherwise I favour the theory of Marinatos, who points out that the Krakatoa eruption, with its much smaller crater of only 22.8 kilometres, caused tidal waves twenty-seven metres high, devastated the coasts of Java and Sumatra, and was responsible for the loss of 36,000 lives. Now Thera is only one hundred kilometres north of Crete, but at one point the sea reaches a depth of over 1800 metres, so that the tidal waves of the Cycladic earthquake should have been considerably higher and more frequent than those of Krakatoa.

A Cycladic settlement on Thera, with pottery imitating Late Minoan I types, was overwhelmed and buried in the debris from this earthquake, and it is not unnatural to suppose that the island and coastal settlements on the north of Crete, such as the harbour town of Knosos, Amnisos, Nirou Khani, Mallia and Gournia were destroyed at the same time or shortly afterwards by the tidal waves and earthquakes.

Marinatos had supposed that Knosos had escaped serious destruction by reason of its greater height and distance from the sea, but I think the palace may have been destroyed by earthquake and fire at that time, even though it may have escaped the tidal waves.

The absence of the Late Minoan II culture (1450–1400 B.C.) from sites other than Knosos, except for an occasional import, can now be better explained by the presence of an Achaean dynasty at Knosos, rather than by assuming that Knosos persisted later than the other Cretan cities . . ."

Such a terrible disaster must have had considerable psychological impact on the Minoans, much as the Lisbon earthquake of A.D. 1755 affected thinking men throughout contemporary Europe. Apart from the violent earthshocks and noise, the secondary marine effects are very impressive. Descriptions by eyewitnesses record that usually the sea recedes, leaving a large expanse of ocean bed exposed, with fish and other marine detritus stranded. After a short time, the sea returns as a mountainous wall of water, overwhelming everything in its path.

Then the waters again draw back, leaving behind the marine life, which has been swept ashore by the tidal waves, mingled together with the wrecks of ships and debris of buildings and occupants destroyed by the onrush of water. Indeed the Minoans must have regarded the cataclysm as a token of divine displeasure which would have found artistic expression, perhaps both to record the vivid impression and simultaneously to placate the gods involved, Poseidon, the god of earthquakes and waters,[3] or another. I believe that this event may indeed have found its expression in the "Marine" style pottery of the Late Minoan Ib period (1500–1450 B.C.) which is described by Hutchinson[4] as corresponding:

> ". . . to the first half of the Late Helladic II period on the mainland and is characterized by pottery with designs of fishes, seaweed, etc., at Knosos and Gournia, Palaikastro and Zakros, but it would be a mistake to assume that it everywhere succeeded the floral and spiral design of Late Minoan Ia . . . This marine style was never very common and was probably a local style either of Knosos or of some eastern site since we do not find it at Mallia, and only rare examples of it at Phaistos . . . Finest of all the Late Minoan Ib vases is the stirrup jar (so called because the false neck with a handle on each side bears a vague resemblance to a stirrup) from Gournia, with a terrifying fiercely alive octopus writhing all over the body of the vase . . . The marine ornaments, which are particularly rich on the rhyta of eastern Crete, comprise octopods, whorl shells, nautilus, starfish and a rock formation looking rather like coral (but certainly nothing of the sort)."

It is significant that this pottery is rare or absent at sites which we could expect to have been destroyed by the tidal waves. The Mycenaeans must have regarded these waves as their allies, as a blessing not a disaster, and may even have come to look upon Poseidon as their patron deity. Perhaps the "Marine" representations from Mycenaean centres are more idealized and less terrifying than those for instance from Gournia, which was disastrously affected. Hutchinson[5] remarks:

> ". . . it is easier to find examples of Late Minoan II vases in the far east . . . than at sites further west, and there is some evidence

there of an Achaean settlement. Perhaps the Eteo-Cretans . . . were 'quislings', glad possibly to escape from the heavy hand of Minoan Mallia, and therefore perhaps not unwilling to establish friendly relations with the new Achaean power at Knosos. There is not much evidence on this point, but there is at least a faint suggestion that the east end of the island was relatively prosperous and on friendly terms with Knosos."

If this speculation about "Marine" pottery is sound it would appear more reasonable to date the catastrophe and the succeeding Mycenaean occupation to the first half of the 15th century, rather than the second. Moreover, Schachermeyr has expressed the view that the alteration of dress shown by the Cretan envoys depicted in the tomb of Rekhmere reflects the conquest of Knossos by Mainland Greeks between 1470–1460 B.C.[6] However, it is proposed to take the date as *c* 1450 B.C., the average of the dates suggested by Hutchinson and Marinatos, which agrees with the authority of Hammond[7] that:

"A Greek dynasty established itself at Cnossus about 1450 and ruled over Crete . . ."

and with Hutchinson's[8] own view:

"that an Achaean dynasty may have ruled over Knosos in the Late Minoan II period from 1450 to 1400 B.C. approximately."

Yet the tidal waves must have had far more serious consequences than a mere temporary influence on pottery styles. Evidence of such a great wave has been found on the northern coast of Crete.[9] It was often the custom of the Minoans to locate their harbours on small promontories[10] to take advantage of the shelter on either side, depending on the wind. Whether the ships were at anchor or drawn up on the beaches, waves of such magnitude must have utterly destroyed all of them on this coast. Thus both the Minoan supremacy in trade, and their protection from invasion, were destroyed at one blow. Hutchinson[11] suggests that, as in Elizabethan times, the Minoan warship was simply a merchant ship with fighting men and that if any fleet existed, it would have been intended to protect the merchant ships from pirates and not to protect the coasts. But to conclude that a powerful merchant fleet with a stiffening of fighting ships was no protection to the island coast would be as big a mistake as that made by Philip of Spain and the Armada. Indeed, with the growth of a mainland sea power, there is archaeological evidence that Mycenaean trade expanded parallel with the Minoan during the early part of the 15th century, rivalled it around 1450[12] and displaced it thereafter.[13] It was also around this time that Cretan fashions of dress began to change, apparently influenced by the Mycenaeans, a new type of kilt without codpiece becoming fashionable, as can be seen in surviving Cretan frescoes.

Many of the inhabitants of the rich coastal cities would have died in the disaster, and there could have been no government. Many of the fighting men would have been drowned, and the flooding of the coastal areas would have made them, at least temporarily, unfit for the exercise of the Minoan chariotry, on such a quagmire strewn with debris. The mainland would have seized its opportunity and used its ships for a successful piratical raid in force on the immobilized Minoan ports, a raid which became a permanent occupation. The local population would have been unable to resist, their physical resources dissipated, their ties of government disrupted, and, in the state of apathy which follows such a disaster, they would have believed that the gods had deserted them. Of course, the tidal waves must have affected the mainland ports and shipping, but the nearest coast there is nearly three times as far away as the northern coast of Crete from the centre of disturbance, and the ports are more sheltered, so that destruction would have been far less. Moreover, from the Linear B tablets from Pylos and Homer's "Catalogue" of the Achaean sea power, we can be sure that the Mycenaean confederation could draw upon ships from Pylos and other centres which had escaped destruction. It appears most likely that the invasion, and the fall of Knossos, followed the eruption immediately, with trade rivalry and the riches of the Minoan cities as powerful motives.

Current opinion is almost unanimous that the Mycenaeans occupied Crete about 1450, but the most serious controversy is how long they controlled the island. Palmer[14] has told this fascinating story, but it may be summarized here. Evans and the traditional school maintained the view that Mycenae represented a branch of Minoan culture and that

Knossos remained Minoan until its destruction *c* 1400 B.C. After this the palace was occupied by squatters—the so-called Reoccupation Period. On the other hand, Wace and Blegen in 1939 advanced the theory that the mainland control over Crete established in Late Minoan II was ended at the time of the destruction of the palace of Knossos *c* 1400 B.C. by a Cretan revolt against the Mycenaean overlords. In 1952 Ventris' brilliant decipherment of the Linear B tablets from Pylos and Knossos proved that they were written in "Mycenaean" Greek. Later, Linear B tablets were found by Wace himself at Mycenae, and Linear B inscriptions had also been found on "stirrup vases" and fragments[15] found at Thebes, Eleusis, Tiryns and Mycenae. These vases may well have contained perfumed oil, possibly as presents sent from one place to another.[16] Palmer has succeeded in identifying Cretan place-names, which also appear in Knossian tablets, in a number of these inscriptions from all these sites on the mainland.[17] Evans himself dated these finds later than the fall of the palace at Knossos, and other experts have subsequently dated these stirrup vases as Late Helladic III or IIIb, consequently:

> "Given this dating, it will be seen that a squatter period at Knossos cannot be reconciled with the evidence presented by the inscribed jars at so many mainland sites. Their wide distribution suggests that Crete as late as 1200 B.C., so far from having no attractions for the mainlander, was in contact with the major Mycenaean centres."

A striking contribution to this problem of the inscribed stirrup-jars from Thebes has just been made by Catling and Millett.[18] By analyzing the composition of a small sample of clay taken from each of the jars, and in particular by determining the content of the "trace element" germanium, they have been able to demonstrate that a considerable proportion (18 out of 25) of the jars examined were made from clay of east Cretan and *not* of Theban origin. The most interesting feature of this discovery is that the source of the jars, which were inscribed when they were manufactured, can almost certainly be attributed to *eastern* Crete and not to Knossos. The fact that they were inscribed when manufactured proves that Linear B script was in use in that part of the island at the date that they were made. Twelve of the jars had "type

F" composition, distinguished by a very low calcium and magnesium content, which is associated with the ancient Minoan site of Zakros. Six others have a "type O" composition which has been located at Palaikastro, also in eastern Crete. Clays from Thebes and Knossos showed a different composition altogether, both being "type B", but the former could be distinguished from the latter by the presence of the trace element germanium.

Unfortunately considerable doubt has been thrown on the possibility of dating these jars with precision.[19] The original excavator, Keramopoullos, placed the destruction of the find building as early as the fourteenth century B.C., and Furumark—the recognized authority on the dating of Mycenaean pottery—dated it to the ceramic phase Mycenaean IIIa-1 (*c* 1425–1400 B.C.), more than 25 years ago. More recently Raison has been said to favour a date at the end of the thirteenth century B.C. for the jars. Recent excavations at Thebes, during 1963–64, have shown that there were probably two later major destructions: one attributed to *c* 1300 B.C., and the other, of a building constructed on the ruins of the former, placed about thirty years later. The earlier building is reported to be on the same orientation as the one in which Keramopoullos found the stirrup-jars, and close to it so that "it might have been a southward extension of it". If so, there would be a strong presumption that the two parts of the building were destroyed at the same time, *c* 1300 B.C. Therefore Platon's date of *c* 1300 B.C. for the destruction of the southern portion of the building would appear to be indicated for the stirrup-jars also. Against this view has to be set the earlier dating postulated by Furumark, and the evidence of the frescoes found in an adjoining room. Catling and Millett note that these may have been painted as early as the second half of the fifteenth century B.C., and that they had been retouched once before the destruction. The comment is made that it is not possible to decide on the length of time that old wall decorations would have been allowed to remain before complete renewal. However, in reaching an opinion on this delicate question I think we can be guided to some extent by the experience of other excavations. It is, perhaps, significant that the date of execution of frescoes found in the palace of Knossos, whose destruction was dated by Evans to the beginning of the fourteenth century B.C., was attributed to the Late Minoan 1a period (1550–1500 B.C.).

Evidently it was quite usual for the Minoans and Mycenaeans to keep such works of art for 150 years or more; so, bearing in mind that this Theban fresco had been retouched, it would seem that any weight of evidence to be attributed to it would be towards the later date (*c* 1300 B.C.) rather than the earlier one.

Further support for this view has been furnished since this book was commenced by the discovery of an important hoard of more than thirty cylinder seals of Babylonian type, which was uncovered in the later building referred to above, whose destruction had been attributed by Platon to *c* 1270 B.C. This find, on the site of the ancient hilltop citadel at Thebes called the Cadmeia after its legendary founder Cadmus, was excavated under the direction of the well-known Greek archaeologist Dr. N. Platon. Palmer and Gurney comment on this discovery as follows:[20]

> "The discovery of a hoard of cylinder seals in a Mycenaean context on the Cadmeia at Thebes should be highly illuminating for chronology. One of them by a most fortunate chance bears an inscription which can be dated with precision. Its design shows a bearded deity emerging from between two mountain peaks . . . He is evidently the weather god dispensing rain.
>
> The inscription on this seal reads 'Kidin-Marduk, son of Shaili-ma-damqa, officer of Burraburiash, King of the World'. This is the name of the owner of the seal. Now Burraburiash was the name of at least two, possibly three, kings of the Third (Kassite) Dynasty of Babylon; but only the last can be considered as the king whose name appears on this seal, since only he laid claim to the title 'King of the World' . . . He ruled for twenty-eight years, roughly from 1381 to 1354 B.C. Thus the seal could not have been made before 1381 B.C. . . . But it is clear that it could hardly have reached its final resting-place before about 1375 B.C.; the date of its deposit is likely to be considerably (perhaps many decades) later than this."

The destruction associated with the stirrup-jars took place about thirty years before that which encapsulated the cylinders, so that the *earliest* likely date for the jars would be *c* 1405 B.C., and the probable date many decades later. The weight of evidence would appear to

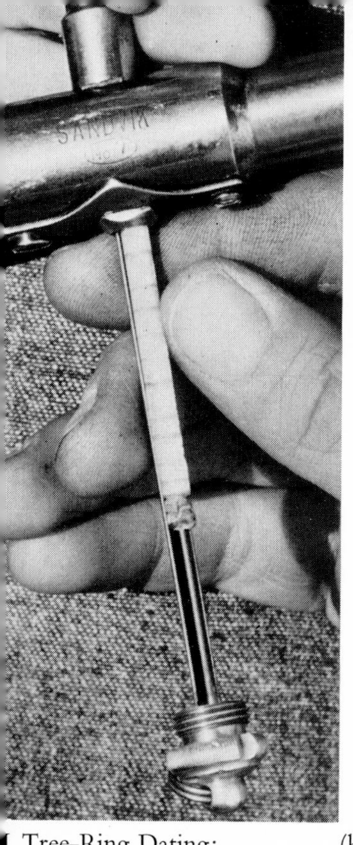

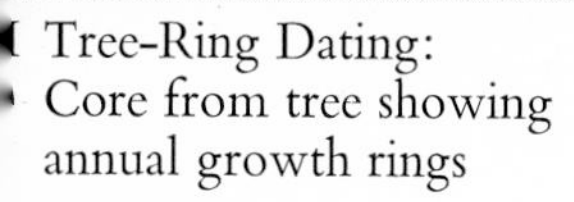
Tree-Ring Dating:
Core from tree showing
annual growth rings

(b) Typical chart of tree rings: A.D. 500 to the present

Photographs by William Belknap Jr.

II Rock Carving of Grecian Galley: Lindos Acropolis

III Island of Carpathos—Stepping Stone to Crete

IV The Northern Entrance Passage: Palace of Knossos

confirm that these jars, inscribed with Linear B script and of east Cretan origin, must have left Crete well after the date usually attributed to the destruction of the Palace at Knossos. It appears that Crete, and by inference Knossos, continued as a flourishing Mycenaean centre *after* 1400 B.C. and that Linear B script continued to be used after that date in Crete.

The finding of this hoard of Babylonian seals also provides striking confirmation of the legendary association of Thebes with the Middle East through Cadmus and Phoenicia (see Chapter 9). It would be reasonable to assume that a Theban dynasty with Phoenician ties would have acquired such a hoard, either as family heirlooms kept in the palace store-rooms or as part of their trade with that area.

All this new evidence adds up to a strong presumption, although not a positive proof, that these Theban stirrup-jars should be dated well *after* the beginning of the fourteenth century B.C., the date assigned by Evans to the destruction of the Palace at Knossos.

Palmer believes that the falls of Pylos (*c* 1200 B.C.) and of Knossos[21] were contemporaneous and were the work of the Dorians,[22] that the correspondence of Knossian culture with that of the mainland Late Helladic III period persisted to the end of that period, and that . . .

> "the dynasts of Knossos during this period (1400) were in effective control of the whole island. So far from being a miserable 'squatter' culture in scattered and isolated sites, they could vie with the lords of Mycenaean Greece at the height of their power."

He has produced[22] a massive body of evidence to support this, some of it taken from the original records of the excavations at Knossos. The controversy turns on the date of the destruction of the Palace of Minos: was it *c* 1400 B.C. or *c* 1200 B.C. as claimed by Palmer and others? His critics have not generally dealt in detail with his factual points, which if not specifically refuted deserve to be accepted. On one occasion where refutation was attempted, it can be shown that the argument cannot be sustained against Palmer. The so-called "Great Deposit of Tablets" was found in the Northern Entrance Passage, intermingled with large numbers of couple-amphorae. The tablets were clustered close against the outside wall of the palace and in Palmer's words:[23]

"This can mean only that they were deposited in this position by a virtually vertical fall from a room over the portico. Any toppling from a room within the exterior wall would have scattered them further into the entrance passage."

Now Evans[24] himself had indicated the "find spot" on a "clearly defined" LM III surface. The couple-amphorae are dated to the LM III period, and in another stratum had been found with a stirrup-jar "of a type marking the extreme period of the Reoccupation". However, Evans dated these tablets *c* 1400 B.C.[24] This date would involve the awkward and unlikely theory[25] that the tablets, written *c* 1400, (and then stored in gypsum boxes with official sealings) must have been deposited by chance—for instance by looters—in the same location as the pottery about 200 years later, at the end of the Reoccupation Period, when the palace was finally abandoned. Palmer assigns the tablets to the LM III period, primarily because they were found with pottery of that period, but he produces other evidence and finally makes the incisive point:

"We recall that the boxes were tied with cord on which the sealings were impressed. It is reasonable to suppose that the fire which destroyed the LM II palace and baked the tablets also affected the string, with the consequence that the sealings fell off. The 'plunderer' hypothesis . . . would involve the assumption that the looters also carried the sealings into the Northern Entrance passage. It would seem simpler to accept the facts as we find them. The whole of this northern deposit of tablets has a clear LM III milieu . . ."

Yet Palmer's critics[26] have claimed that the tablets cannot belong to the same period as the LM III pottery with them in the deposit, because any pottery present at the time the palace was destroyed by fire must have been burnt, too, but this pottery shows no signs of fire. This criticism cannot be sustained; any amateur strategist who has known two World Wars can see that the area round the Northern Entrance Passage is precisely where the conquerors would have brought supplies after burning and looting the palace. They would have camped in the ruins, and used the Central Court as parade and assembly ground. The high points on either side of the passage (see Plate IV) are the most likely places for the main lookout posts, as they command the surrounding countryside and the old paved Minoan road to the port of Amnisos, where their fleet must have been. Victorious soldiers are notoriously free with captured enemy stores; no doubt they brought them in through this passage from the unburnt parts of the city, for example, from the nearby magazines of the Little Palace, which according to Evans survived unburnt until the end of the Reoccupation Period.[27]

Whether the couple-amphorae contained oil and wine for the inward, or perfumed friction oil for the outward, gratification of the victors, there is a good reason why the empties were deposited at one end of the northern passage. This was the main and most vulnerable way into the palace; the temporary garrison, needing to obstruct any rush of armed men who might make a surprise counter-attack, chose couple-amphorae (see Plate V) which made excellent "caltrops". The inventive Dorians might indeed be credited with inventing this defensive weapon. Readily movable, the couple-amphorae could have been piled at one side of the passage and used at night or against a surprise attack, as a carpet of "caltrops". They would have slowed any onrush of soldiers, jostling them in the narrow passage and exposing them to Dorian fire above and on either side (see Plate IV). Those who penetrated the obstruction would have been thrown off balance and vulnerable to spearmen and swordsmen on the inside of it. This theory is supported by evidence mentioned by Boardman[28] who cites Evans and Mackenzie as reporting that late blocking walls were found at the outer end of the passage.

Plate VI, a photograph of Evans' excavations in 1900, shows clearly that *as excavated* this blocking wall only restricted its width and did not block it entirely. Two further blocking walls of late construction had also been added further to the north at some time, and these definitely do not close off the approaches, but only act as "baffles".[29] Evans and Pendlebury had interpreted the results of their excavations as showing that the passageway had been widened by dismantling the outer wall of the East Bastion—the top part of which is clearly visible in Plate VI in the centre of the floor of the passage—leaving only the inner wall (visible in the centre of Plate VI). However, Boardman[30] considers that at this time there was:

> "still a construction of some sort over the outer wall of the East Bastion. It seems then that the passage between the bastions was walled off at the north in the Re-occupation period and used perhaps as a store . . ."

It seems clear that such "diversion" walls were added to supplement the caltrop barrier. They were quite makeshift, and could well have been added by the Dorians in the later part of their temporary occupation, or even later by squatters as a defence, though their date is unknown.

This explanation seems more likely than that they formed the walls of a squatters' store. There is no evidence of any roof-fall; Boardman says:

> "the intact vases are undamaged by anything falling on them, let alone anything burning."

There would be little point in an unroofed store, particularly in a passageway with so many nearby rooms available. The passage slopes down to the north steeply, so a complete blocking wall would have dammed up water running down from the main court and flooded the store-room.

All this evidence indicates a short occupation. Could it have been an interlude before moving on to Pylos and the mainland? This question will be examined further in Chapter 8 when considering the role of the Dorians in Crete.

We can thus account for the presence of vases (*c* 1200 B.C.) unmarked by fire in the Northern Entrance Passage, while the tablets' position is consistent with a fall from a room above when the palace was burnt. The position and condition of both tablets and vases is not only readily explained, but fits exactly with what we could expect when the palace was fired and sacked.

We are still left with the difficulty of explaining why so much LM III pottery was found in association with earlier LM II/IIIa ware in so many locations in the palace of Knossos. I think that an explanation for this may be found in the effects of the volcanic disaster which decimated the island, and in those of the subsequent Mycenaean invasion (*c* 1450 B.C.), coupled with the fact that the new rule was more broadly based than the Minoan which preceded it (Chapter 11). The former event would have damaged the agricultural wealth of the country, leaving a smaller share of it available to be devoted to the production of luxury pottery, while the conquerors would undoubtedly have favoured the diversion of some of the most skilled craftsmen to the mainland. Moreover, the conquest would have led to less demand for the finest pottery because the new ruler would probably have been a governor, or at the most a viceroy owing allegiance to the mainland —as is indicated by Homer at the time of the Trojan War.

There does seem to have been a tendency to equate the level of civilization too strictly with the "pots" rather than to link them also with the political background, and the degree of taste and sophistication prevailing in a particular period. At this point we should recall Thucydides' well-known warning to future generations that they would be grossly misled if they were to assess the relative power of Sparta and Athens by the remains of their ancient cities, a comment which was based on similar considerations. People with poor pots are not necessarily wild and uncivilized; this manifestation may merely reflect a wider distribution of wealth and a more democratic way of life with a tendency towards mass production to meet the needs arising from it.

Following the Mycenaean invasion, therefore, one would expect that the existing styles at the time of the invasion, which in any case were evidently admired by them, would have continued in production with some degeneration in style because of the decline in wealthy patronage. Therefore, if the destruction of the Palace is attributed to the Dorians, we would expect to find a mixture of pottery styles in the ruins. This would comprise pre-invasion pottery of the Minoans (LM II/LM IIIa) in conjunction with later LM III ware influenced by the Mycenaean invaders covering the period *c* 1450 B.C. to the time of the destruction of the Palace. The Minoan pottery would consist of pre-invasion masterpieces preserved in the Palace, and elsewhere, after the Mycenaean take-over, and of similar ware—often of poorer quality —which had continued in production during an extended period of Mycenaean rule. In fact we postulate for Crete, and Knossos in particular, the same thesis that is freely accepted for other archaeological sites: that the pottery of the intrusive element continued side by side with that of the indigenous culture.

This is exactly the situation revealed in some of the areas of the Palace at Knossos by the excavations. Because the new occupants of the Palace were Mycenaean feudalists, rather than the court of a king-emperor, they would have retained many of the existing *objets d'art* of the former regime to embellish the Government House into which it was converted. The new ruling element in Crete would have consisted of younger sons, adventurers and *nouveaux riches* who had been brought up to admire Minoan culture, so that there would have been every reason for production of the finer pottery to continue in the same style, albeit with some deterioration. Ware produced for current day-to-day use would, however, have been more utilitarian than the former royal Minoan product, hence the later LM III product which is generally referred to as "degenerate".

It is this simpler style of pottery which, hitherto, has generally been attributed to the "squatters". This situation would have covered the period of Mycenaean rule *c* 1450–1192 B.C., and would have been succeeded by the Dark Ages, which followed the disruptions and pestilence resulting from the Dorian invasions. Of course, after the final fall of the Palace, whether this took place during a landing in Crete *c* 1192 B.C. while the Dorians were en route to Pylos, or *c* 1150 B.C. when they returned to occupy the island, we could expect a period of "squatters" in the ruins of the Palace, with their accompanying "intrusive walls" and artifacts. This period would correspond to that of the cities of refuge at Karphi and Vrokastro, with their lower level of culture, and "squatters" in the Palace of Knossos seem to fit much better into that time than they do into the previous phase *c* 1450–1200 B.C., when we now know that Crete was trading in luxury goods with the mainland—as witnessed by the evidence of the Theban stirrup-jars and the tablets of Pylos which record bronze tripods imported from Crete.

Palmer must be right and without reasonable doubt the date of the main destruction of the Palace at Knossos was *c* 1200 B.C and not 1400, while the most likely cause of its downfall was the "Dorians". To support this view, there is one final, even if circumstantial, piece of evidence. Strangely enough, this is concealed in the famous and oft-quoted words of Pendlebury:[31]

> "And in the last decade of the fifteenth century on a spring day, when a strong South wind was blowing which carried the flames of the burning beams almost horizontally northwards, Knossos fell."

Now this is historical, even though it is written in smoke instead of the "syllabary" used in the tablets. It is almost certain that it could not have been the Mycenaeans who burnt and sacked the Palace on this occasion, *because ancient ships of this period could not sail or progress against the wind,* but could only proceed crosswind or with it. So the Mycenaeans could not have sailed southwards from the mainland at a time when a strong wind was blowing from the south—*but such a wind would have aided the Dorians if they were coming from the east.* This wind would also have offered them a good means of escape to northern Thessaly or the Ambracian Gulf should their Cretan raid have been repulsed.

This evidence cannot be regarded as conclusive; for alternative, though less likely, explanations can be given:

1. As Wace suggested, the destruction of the Palace was due to an uprising of the local inhabitants (*c* 1400 B.C.) against their Mycenaean overlords.
2. The Palace fell to invaders who had already landed elsewhere in the island, when the wind was favourable, and who then attacked Knossos overland, thus giving time for the wind to change.
3. The wind changed and started to blow from the south after the invasion had started.

Any one of these explanations is just possible, but the balance of probability is against them. The local uprising theory is not consistent with the flourishing of Cretan trade, particularly exports to the Greek mainland—*c* 1400–1200 B.C.; nor with the Homeric tradition that Idomeneus and a powerful Cretan force were loyal allies to the Mycenaeans at Troy.

The second possibility is highly unlikely, as the customary tactics of ancient times involved a sharp, surprise raid in force from the sea in order to obtain maximum plunder at minimum cost. Moreover, there is clear evidence from the Linear B tablets unearthed at Knossos that there were considerable stocks of chariots and other war materials stored at Knossos, while we can quote from Homer's "Catalogue":

> "And spear-renowned Idomeneus was captain of the Cretans that held Knossos and wall-girt Gortys, Lyctus and Miletus and chalk-white Lycastus, and Phaestos and Rhytium, well-peopled cities, and yet other peoples who dwell in Crete with its hundred cities. Of all of them was spear-renowned Idomeneus captain . . . With them followed eighty black ships."

Against such a strong force anything but a surprise attack would have been a grave tactical error. Moreover, Knossos was the centre of the island's wealth and so the main target for a raid. An overland attack would have given Knossos time to mobilize and concentrate its forces. This would have held true from whatever direction, and at whatever time, the invasion took place. All the archaeological evidence available points to the fact that the Palace fell to a surprise attack. The town was not walled, so no siege took place, and the excavators have found no evidence of prolonged fighting in the Palace itself, indeed, as quoted by Palmer,[32] they interpreted the evidence as indicating that a sudden disaster had taken place:[31]

> "The final scene takes place in the most dramatic room ever excavated—the Throne Room. It was found in a state of complete confusion. A great oil jar lay overturned in one corner, ritual vessels were in the act of being used when the disaster came. It looks as if the king had been hurried here to undergo too late some late ceremony in the hope of saving the people."

It is possible that, if Homer and Staphylos were correct in claiming that Dorians were in eastern Crete before the Trojan War, there could have been a simultaneous revolt in eastern Crete. The leaders of the Dorians, returning from their incursion into Asia Minor and southwards towards Egypt, could have fomented such a revolt by their kinsmen in eastern Crete. By suitably timing this Dorian rising against their overlords at Knossos it would have been possible to draw off a substantial part of the defence force stationed there towards the east. This would have ensured that the City and Palace fell as an easy prey to the invaders from the sea, and that the force dispatched towards the eastern part of the island would have been left without a base for their return, and thus could have been destroyed in detail.

The last possibility, that of a change of wind, is just too much of a coincidence to be likely. We are not dealing here with the milder land and sea breezes, which alternate during the course of the day, but with a strong wind which blew the flames nearly horizontally. The Greeks, Mycenaeans or Dorians, were weatherwise seamen, and would not have attempted an enterprise of such importance unless they were reasonably certain of the weather. It is clear that the attack was short and sharp, so there was little time for a complete change in the weather.

There is one further minor point about the weather.[33] The vivid phrase about the "wild spring day" seems to have crept into the history books, but I am not sure of its origin; I believe that it may possibly be connected with the Greek legend that Theseus sailed for Crete and the labyrinth on a spring morning. The prevailing wind at Knossos blows from the south during December and January; while sometimes in the summer months hot winds, termed the "livas",[34] come up from the African desert. Statistically, therefore, spring would be unlikely for the day of the holocaust, but bearing in mind the navigation season and the indication that the magazines at Knossos were full of the fruits of the harvest, a day in the late summer would, perhaps, be more likely.

We may thus conclude that the evidence from Crete is consistent with a Dorian invasion *c* 1200 B.C., and that this supports the probability of a main initial Dorian attack on the Greek mainland from Asia Minor. The nature and direction of the anticipated attack on Pylos—by sea and from the south—deduced from the Linear B tablets unearthed there—also fit the possibility that Crete, and Knossos in particular, was used as a base or at least a staging-point, though this is not essential; the Dorian fleet proceeding from the ports and islands of the eastern Mediterranean could have by-passed Crete and attacked the Greek mainland direct.

However, they must surely have been prepared to attack Knossos if they were ready to attempt a landing at Pylos. Knossos was a bigger prize, rich in potential plunder, open to a surprise raid—which was less feasible at Pylos. Knossos taken, it could then be used for regrouping the invaders' forces, drawing on the armaments and provisions in the magazines and recruiting or impressing reinforcements from the local Minoans, many of whom would not have been adverse to helping to turn the tables on their Mycenaean overlords.

Finally, there may be some evidence that the invasion of Pylos came from Crete preserved in one of the Delphic "Homeric" hymns. The Greeks were adept at incorporating a nugget of history in an embroidery of legend so that the thin bullion thread of fact stiffened the whole. Thus the hymn written for the priests at Delphi (to quote Seltman's apt condensed version[35]) tells:

> "firstly how Apollo came to Delphi, took it for his own, and then got him Dorians from Crete to be the keepers of his temple. Down from Olympus he came and travelled south through the plains of Thessaly to Iolkos and crossed to Euboea; thence he struck west over the narrows, into Boeotia, and on into the mountains—
>
> 'And thence he went speeding swiftly to the mountain ridge,
> And came to Crisa beneath snowy Parnassus,
> A foot-hill turned towards the west: a cliff hangs
> Over it from above; and a hollow rugged glade runs under.
> There the lord Phoebus Apollo resolved to make his lovely temple,
>
> ....
>
> Then Phoebus Apollo pondered in his heart
> What men he should bring to be his ministers
> In sacrifice and to serve him in rocky Pytho.
> And while he considered, he became aware of a swift ship on the wine-like sea,
> *In which were many men and* goodly Cretans from Cnossos,
> The city of Minos, they who do sacrifice
> To the prince and announce his decrees, whatsoever Phoebus Apollo,
> Bearer of the golden blade, speaks in answer
> From his laurel below the dells of Parnassus.
> *These men were sailing in their black ships* for gain and profit to sandy Pylos,

And to the men of Pylos. But Phoebus Apollo met them:
In the open sea he sprang upon their swift ship, like a dolphin in shape,
And lay there, a great and awesome monster, and none of them gave heed so as to understand,
But they sought to cast the dolphin overboard. But he kept shaking
The black ship every way and making the timbers quiver.'

....

Then in the end he brought them to the port of Delphi in the Corinthian Gulf."

Of course, the hymn does not tell of a walking-tour by Apollo, trying out his seven league boots, but it obviously records the route followed by the army and nation, whose patron deity he was, in their course southward to join their kinsmen in the Peloponnese. The route from Olympus is exactly the route best followed by an invading army. Anyone who has driven along the western shores of the Gulf of Euboea northwards via Lamia to Volos, and has stood on the slopes of Mount Pilion looking across at the north coast of the island of Euboea, cannot fail to be impressed by the potential invasion beaches available. These, coupled with the sheltered Bay of Pagasai in which the Dorian/Thessalian fleet could have assembled, centred on Iolkos, made the route Iolkos-Euboea-Chalcis-Aulis a brilliant strategic choice to by-pass the strong defensive positions at Thermopylae and along the mountainous coast. In this manner the Dorian armies, debouching onto the mainland plains, would have taken Thebes and Orchomenus in the rear, cut them off, and destroyed their forces piecemeal.

All the details are in the above story, including the sacking of Pylos "for gain and profit", Knossos and the Dorians coming from Crete. Even the manifestation of Apollo as a dolphin rings true. Earlier in this chapter it was suggested that for the Mycenaeans, possibly demonstrated by the "Marine" style pottery of the Late Minoan Ib period, Poseidon was the patron deity, and that they regarded the consequences of the tidal wave after the eruption of Thera as a manifestation of his divine support. It is likely that the Dorians would have claimed a similar manifestation for their final overmastering of the Mycenaeans. The italics in the phrase "In which were many men and . . ." are mine. I think this wording is intended to convey that the central ship was accompanied by many others, as is indicated immediately after by the use of the plural. The ships of this time were small and a few ships could hardly be said to accommodate "many men" as well as a number of Cretan priests.

One further point calls for comment: the implication that the voyage from Knossos was also for the gain and profit of the men of Pylos, which seems a strange way of referring to the consequence of the invasion of their land. The hymn was written for the Delphic priests, and religious leaders have often regarded forcible subjection of a people in religious matters as being for their spiritual gain and profit. Also, the significance of Pylos in the Dorian invasion may possibly have been lost by the time the hymn was written; this reference may therefore be an attempt to rationalize the tradition of a voyage when the full details had been lost and the purpose had become obscure. It could all be a coincidence, but if so this passage is a remarkable one.

If the Dorians did not remain in Crete at first, the islanders would no doubt have attempted to recover and carry on as before. But they would have had little opportunity to return to their former prosperity, as almost certainly the Dorians would have raided their coasts from Peloponnesian bases. Further, the respite was short, as tradition records that they returned about 1150 B.C., this time to remain and colonize the rich plains, particularly in the centre of the island.

The dispossessed Mycenaeans and their Cretan retainers, driven into the more inaccessible parts, even set up so-called "Cities of Refuge" on mountainous and easily defensible sites. Two of the most important which have been excavated are Vrokastro and Karphi,[36] situated about 3 miles east of Gournia and 20 miles east-south-east of Knossos respectively. Karphi was evidently the more important, containing a mansion with a megaron of the mainland Mycenaean type, and we can assume this house was the residence of the local ruler. There was a bazaar quarter and a civic shrine with associated priest's house.[36]

These "Cities of Refuge" must have served as rallying centres when the Dorians raided up from the plains, and in them the Mycenaean culture endured, on a much reduced and debased scale. Along with some innovations taken over from their enemies—such as the long bronze pins and fibulae used to fasten the Doric peplos—these refugees carried their pottery styles with them and these sites can be dated from their sherds. The finds at Vrokastro were more abundant and better stratified than at Karphi, and the top level of the town can be dated as *ending* about 1050 B.C. as it contains sub-Minoan sherds.[37] The site at Karphi has been dated *c* 1100–900 B.C. by similar means.[38] These dates fit well with the estimated date of *c* 1150 B.C. for the main Dorian invasion of Crete, particularly when it is realized that for the first few decades after the occupation commenced general chaos would have reigned, and the refugees would not have been able to organize their refuge until it was realized that the Dorians were content with occupying the rich plains. The sites were apparently abandoned peacefully as there is no sign of their having been plundered, and no gold or other valuables were found in Karphi or the tombs associated with it.[39] Hutchinson[40] has suggested, on the evidence of the place-names in Crete, that the classical population of the island must have possessed a large percentage of Minoan blood. This seems to be supported by anthropology, as the original Cretans of the Bronze Age were normally dolichocephalic (long-headed) with a cranial index below 75, while most modern Cretans are of the mesocephalic (medium-headed) type with cranial indices falling within the bracket of 75.0 to 79.9.[41] On the other hand we find that the brachycephalic (broad-headed) type has prevailed in modern Greece, where the normal cranial index is 80 or more.

The dates of occupation of these sites also fit with the evidence that the Dorian occupation *c* 1150 B.C. was confined to the plains, as the occupation of Vrokastro on the basis of its terminal date (*c* 1050) started somewhat earlier and finished considerably earlier (*c* 1050 versus *c* 900) than that at Karphi, which was threatened more closely from the plains which were under Dorian domination. The ties of kinship between the earlier Dorian settlers in the east of Crete and the invaders who arrived *c* 1150 were clearly not sufficient to protect the former from plunder. But when the new arrivals began to be absorbed into the native population, it is evident that the rapprochement was achieved more rapidly in those areas which had been settled by their kin in earlier times. Hence Vrokastro could be vacated for a better site much earlier than Karphi.

With the Dorian element being absorbed into the indigenous population, we must leave Crete since we would otherwise pass outside the period with which we are concerned.

REFERENCES

[1] Hutchinson, R. W., *Prehistoric Crete,* Pelican Books, 1962, p. 300.

[2] Hutchinson, R. W., *ibid,* p. 302.

[3] Palmer, L. R., *Mycenaeans and Minoans,* 1961, p. 129.

[4] Hutchinson, R. W., *ibid,* p. 281f.

[5] Hutchinson, R. W., *ibid,* p. 299.

[6] Review, Journal of Hellenic Studies, 85, (Schachermeyr, F., "Die Minoische Kultur des alten Kreta", W. Kohlhammer, Stuttgart, 1964), p. 229.

[7] Hammond, N. G. L., *A History of Greece to 322 B.C.,* 1959, p. 45.

[8] Hutchinson, R. W., *ibid,* p. 110.

[9] Christoforakis, J. M., *Crete,* 1961, p. 8.

[10] Hutchinson, R. W., *ibid,* p. 100.

[11] Hutchinson, R. W., *ibid,* p. 98f.

[12] Hammond, N. G. L., *ibid,* p. 45; Hutchinson, R. W., *ibid,* p. 110.

[13] Hammond, N. G. L., *ibid,* p. 46f.

[14] Palmer, L. R., *ibid,* p. 158f.

[15] Palmer, L. R., *ibid,* p. 167.

[16] Palmer, L. R., *ibid,* p. 170.

[17] Palmer, L. R., *ibid,* p. 168f.

[18] Catling, H. W. and Millett, A., Archaeometry, 8, 1965, p. 13f.

[19] Catling, H. W. and Millett, A., *ibid,* p. 13f.

[20] Palmer, L. R. and Gurney, O. R., The Times, 17th July, 1964.

[21] Palmer, L. R., *ibid,* p. 166.

[22] Palmer, L. R., *ibid,* p. 207.

[23] Palmer, L. R., *ibid,* p. 220.

[24] Palmer, L. R., *ibid,* p. 192f.

[25] Palmer, L. R., *ibid,* p. 221f.

[26] Boardman, J., *The Date of the Knossos Tablets,* 1963, p. 49.

[27] Palmer, L. R., *ibid,* p. 207.

[28] Boardman, J., *ibid,* pp. 42, 45, 48, Figure 8 and Plate XI.

[29] Boardman, J., *ibid,* p. 42, Figure 8.

[30] Boardman, J., *ibid,* p. 48.

[31] Pendlebury, J. D. S., *The Archaeology of Crete,* 1939, p. 231.

[32] Palmer, L. R., *ibid,* p. 160.

[33] Pendlebury, J. D. S., *A Handbook to the Palace of Minos, Knossos,* 1954, p. 36.

[34] Christoforakis, J. M., *ibid*, pp. 19–20.

[35] Seltman, C., *The Twelve Olympians*, Pan Books, 1961, p. 125.

[36] MacKendrick, P., *The Greek Stones Speak*, 1962, pp. 136–40; Desborough, V. R. d'A., *The Last Mycenaeans and Their Successors*, 1964, p. 194.

[37] MacKendrick, P., *ibid*, p. 140.

[38] MacKendrick, P., *ibid*, p. 137.

[39] MacKendrick, P., *ibid*, p. 137.

[40] Hutchinson, R. W., *ibid*, p. 319.

[41] Hutchinson, R. W., *ibid*, p. 59.

CHAPTER SIX

"The Wars of the Roses"

Now is the winter of our discontent
Made glorious summer

SHAKESPEARE

THE picture of the social organization depicted in the Linear B tablets, the Homeric sagas and the Greek traditions, is one of a proto-feudal society similar to the structure of the German tribes described by Roman writers, and of the early European Middle Ages recorded in our own histories. There is the central figure of a "King of Men" to whom the other kings in the Mycenaean federation owed a loose allegiance, which became stricter under the stress of war or the incentive of united plundering; the employment of mercenaries was also common. In this pattern are all the elements which led to our own "Wars of the Roses".

> ". . . Though two major Mycenaean centres allegedly went down in ruin, one at the end of the fifteenth century and the other shortly after, it was precisely the following century and a half that saw the greatest expansion of Mycenaean power and influence . . ."[1]

Palmer made the tentative suggestion that the destruction of the Palaces of Knossos and Thebes was a result of a Greek "Wars of the Roses" between these two powers and a Mycenaean confederation. He came to the conclusion that, for Knossos, it gave rise to "difficulties no less severe than it would solve" because it was unlikely that the rich island of Crete would have been subsequently abandoned by the Mycenaean victors after the destruction of Knossos—which was the then current view—and because his own researches led him later to the conclusion that the Knossian Linear B tablets were roughly contemporary with those of Pylos (*c* 1200 B.C.). As a result of Marinatos' theory we reach the conclusion (Chapter 5) that the Mycenaean

V Couple-Amphorae from Knossos Photograph: Ashmolean Museum

VI Knossos Excavations A.D. 1900: The Northern Entrance Passage
Photograph: Ashmolean Museum

VII Mycenae, "Warrior Vase", *c* 12th century B.C.

VIII Terracotta Frieze of Phrygian Warriors
Photograph from Seton Lloyd: *Early Anatolia* (Penguin)

conquest of Crete (*c* 1450 B.C.) was rather the material consequence of the catastrophic eruption of the island of Thera that the latter postulates. This caused Crete to fall as a ripe plum to the Mycenaean confederation. However, by a slight modification of Palmer's interesting suggestion, I believe that the background can be shown logically to link up with Homeric and other Greek tradition and with the events following the fall of Troy.

This hypothesis (Theory 7 in Chapter 3) of a war of north and east with south and west is, of course, highly speculative. There is little direct evidence, the main support coming from the Homeric "Catalogues" and a few scattered references in the Hittite records.

The fall of Thebes, to the attack launched under the leadership of the Epigoni, is dated[2] approximately one generation before the Trojan War, i.e. around 1280 B.C., if we accept Blegen's date[3] of *c* 1250 B.C. for the sack of Troy VIIa. There seems to be no evidence that Troy had been involved in active hostilities at the time of the attack on Thebes. It was not until *c* 1230 that a falling off in Mycenaean exports of pottery[4] to Syria, Palestine and Egypt took place, presumably the result of either the Trojan War itself or its aftermath, notably the failure of the expedition against Egypt *c* 1221 B.C. with all its repercussions, so it is unlikely that this date could be pushed back sufficiently to coincide with the Theban War. It would therefore appear that this hypothesis would have to be constructed on the basis that Thebes was eliminated well before Troy and its allies were involved in active hostilities with the Mycenaean confederation, and the part that Thebes played in the affair was possibly to furnish a few dispossessed grandees as refugees to the camp of the Trojan allies, including the Heracleidae, who ultimately returned at the head of the Dorian invaders to cause the ruin of their Mycenaean enemies.

In this connection there is one interesting aside in Herodotus,[5] when he is referring to the naval victory of the Phocaeans over the Tyrrhenians and Carthaginians off Sardinia. Herodotus refers to the battle as "*a Cadmeian sort of victory with more loss than gain*". It is tempting to see in this comment a reference to the opening stages of the Greek "Wars of the Roses", and a realization that the fall of the Cadmeian city of Thebes, while apparently a victory for the central Mycenaean power, set in train consequences which led to its ultimate downfall.

The general background emerging from this speculation, formed mainly from the Greek legends, indicates that the formation of the Mycenaean confederation was catalyzed by the fall of Crete to their arms, as a result of the disruption caused by the fortuitous eruption on the island of Thera. The access of the wealth and power of Crete to this loose confederation of mainland states had an important influence. Rivalry sprang up and led, amongst other incidents, to the expulsion of the Achaean clan of the Heracleidae and the fall of Thebes. We do not know whether Troy was actually part of the confederation, or an ally or merely friendly. To speculate that Troy was at some stage part of this association would be in accordance with the interpretation of the Hittite records[6] of the end of the fourteenth century which evidently refer to two Achaean kings, one the king of the Greek mainland, the other a local king who owed some sort of allegiance to his mainland overlord. It would also fit in with the old tradition[7] of a Grecian "Thalassocracy" in the Aegean, and with the indications of Mycenaean settlements tentatively dated to this period, which have been discovered on the mainland of Asia Minor over recent years (see Chapter 2). A common origin has been postulated for the Trojans and the Greeks and this is dealt with in more detail below (Chapter 7). The counter-argument advanced that this view is not sustainable because of the philological evidence, can perhaps be explained and this aspect is also dealt with later (Chapter 7). If this common origin is accepted, the inclusion of Troy in the Mycenaean confederation, either as an ally or actual member, is a plausible assumption. It would fit in with the close trade links, which explain the Hittite records referred to above, and the Mycenaean pottery finds in Troy itself and in some of the settlements tentatively dated before the fall of Troy which have been discovered in recent years along the eastern Mediterranean coast.

The main support for the speculation that a "Wars of the Roses" broke out between the Trojans and their allies and a Mycenaean confederation centred on the Argolid, lies in the Homeric "Catalogues" of the forces which fought on the opposing sides in the Trojan War, quoted in the *Iliad*. There is a strong body of opinion amongst current authorities that these catalogues are historical records of the conditions prevailing at the time of the Trojan War, which had been handed down by word of mouth and incorporated in the *Iliad* as a tradition important to the feudal aristocracy for whose entertainment such epic sagas were composed. It is believed that very little interpolation and alteration occurred in these Catalogues,[8] which the Greeks regarded as an authentic historical record of their past which was sacrosanct and safe from mutilation in much the same way as Shakespeare's works and the Bible have been. Athens plays a relatively minor role;[8] yet because of her political and literary dominance during the classical period, she was in a unique position to amend the Catalogue in her favour.

The composition of the Trojan host is given in these Catalogues as:

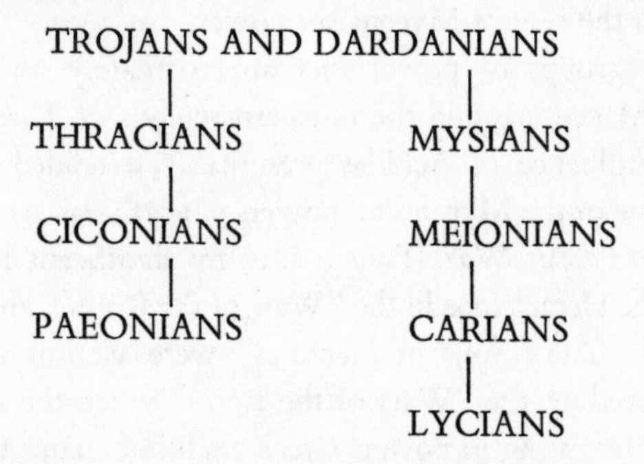

It will be noted that, leaving on one side the Paphlagonians, Alizones and Phrygians located away from the Aegean coastline, all the other peoples are arranged in order starting from Troy as the focal point and extending outwards to the valley of the Axios, and southwards to Lycia on the Syrian border. This order is similar to the form of presentation remarked on by Palmer,[9] used in Pylian Linear B tablets to record the geographical relationships of the coastal bases in the Messenian peninsula which terminates in Cape Akritas. It was also used by the geographer Strabo later to record the place-names here. However, the order of presentation then started at each end of the arc and finished at the focal point Cape Akritas.

The presentation of the Achaean host is roughly similar but less marked, with the Argolid as the focal point and the sequence of the contingents radiating out in two closed loops like a distorted figure of eight centred on Mycenae (see Figure 4, front endpapers). After the main lists we find a further long list of associated members of the confederation, starting with Crete and Rhodes. Hammond[10] has conjectured that this order may be traditional. It would be interesting to know whether it gives any clue to the sequence of growth of the Mycenaean empire. The southern loop lies in the heart of the Catalogue, is preceded by the northern loop and followed by a long list of miscellaneous kingdoms such as Crete and Rhodes, on the periphery of the empire. This order seems to approximate to our understanding of the growth of the Mycenaean confederation. One feature is noteworthy: Thebes is not included, but significantly the lower town of Thebes (Hypothebia) is named.[8] This is precisely what we would expect after Thebes had been overmastered, and the kingdoms subordinated to the central Mycenaean power.

The two groups of power met approximately on the southern borders of Macedonia and the northern regions of Thessaly, towards which the influence of Achilles presumably extended as the ruling representative of the Mycenaean powers in north-eastern Greece at the time of the Trojan War. Two points are significant here: the part played by the Heracleidae in the "Wars of the Roses", and the "Wrath of Achilles". The "Sons of Hercules" were victims of the power struggle preceding the "Wars of the Roses" when the Argolid kingdoms were increasing in power. Greek tradition claims that the "Sons of Hercules" returned with the Dorians, and as Tiryns is traditionally associated with the name of Hercules, it can be inferred that they were dispossessed during the prologue to the "Wars of the Roses" and took refuge possibly first in Thebes and later with the less civilized tribes in the north and north-east of Greece, in this borderland between the Mycenaean and Trojan factions. It can be assumed that two or three generations after the war, between their flight from the Argolid and their return, they played an important role in organizing the Dorians, whom tradition emphasizes they led. It is even possible that some of the Heracleidae took refuge in Asia Minor and participated in the war on the Trojan side. Asia Minor was the traditional refuge for political fugitives in the later classical period.

There is just one slight indication in the Greek tradition recorded by Herodotus that Hyllus, one of the "Sons of Hercules", was killed in a duel at the Isthmus of Corinth during an attempted invasion by the Dorians; as a result of this defeat, they announced they would not return for three generations. However, this incident is traditionally dated to the generation before the Trojan War. The discrepancy could perhaps be explained if the tradition had been slightly corrupted and originally referred to the generation preceding the fall of Troy, which would place it near the opening stages of the Trojan War. This is, of course, pure speculation. It appears most unlikely that the Dorians would have attempted to attack the Mycenaean kingdoms one generation before the Trojan War, when the latter were at the height of their power. An attempt was much more likely in the opening stages of the war when the fighting power of these kingdoms would have been operating in the eastern Aegean and the Argolid itself was stripped of fighting men.

However, there is a reference in the *Iliad,* and Greek tradition, that one of the "Sons of Hercules" participated in the war on the Achaean side: Tlepolemus led the marine contingent from Rhodes. In our own "Wars of the Roses" members of noble houses frequently participated on opposite sides in the struggle, so Tlepolemus was presumably one of the more fortunate of the noble "Sons of Hercules" who by good fortune was able to remain on good terms with the Mycenaean rulers and maintain his feudal overlordship at Rhodes.

Apart from the Hyllus incident, there is no evidence that the Heracleidae played much part in the fighting at Troy. This may be because Homer composed his saga from older epics constructed for the entertainment of Mycenaean nobility whose ancestors had fought at Troy; accordingly they passed over the Heracleidae since they could be regarded as Mycenaean renegades. This explanation is not very convincing, and it would seem more likely that the Heracleidae bided their time until their enemies were weakened by the attrition of the Trojan War, and its resulting rivalries. We shall probably never know the answer, but whether or not the "Sons of Hercules" participated it is certain they would have directed their efforts to stirring up trouble between the two factions, and by organizing the tribes among whom they had settled they would have prepared for the day when they could take their revenge. For this they were in a strong position, familiar as they were with the bureaucratic organization and technical skills of the Mycenaeans and Minoans.

The "Wrath of Achilles" may also have a deeper significance beyond that apparently given it by Homer at first sight. The epic opens on this theme and carries it through the whole story with consummate artistry, bringing out the consequences of greed and pride which led to the climax of the death of Patroclus, and the downfall of Hector at the hands of Achilles, the beginning of the end for Troy. Now the Grecian bardic legends, and the writings of Hesiod, looked back with nostalgia to a Golden Age which was succeeded by the Heroic Period and ended by the Age of Iron, and Homer centres the *Iliad* on the "Wrath of Achilles" and its consequences rather than on the downfall of Troy itself. It would appear most unlikely that the breach between Agamemnon and the clan of Achilles was healed by the fall of Troy, nor that the resentment felt by the latter was assuaged by the murder of their enemy. The breach between the two noble houses would almost certainly have been handed on, and ultimately would have been a major contribution to the subsequent disintegration of the Mycenaean empire.

After the actual fall of Troy, audiences hearing these sagas or the *Iliad* would have been conscious of the part played by the main characters in bringing disaster to themselves and their friends, apart from the destruction of Troy itself. But surely Homer and perhaps some of his audience would have appreciated the effect of the greed and pride of Agamemnon and the pride and anger of Achilles on the downfall of the Mycenaean empire. This brought the end of the Golden Age when their ancestry had controlled the wealth and trade of the Aegean and beyond, and ushered in the Age of Iron when chaos and destruction were rife.

The fall of Troy would not have brought an end to the rift. The kingdoms of Achilles bordered on the area where the Dorians are traditionally thought to have resided at that time,[11] and they had been displaced first from Phthiotis and later from the rich vale of Tempe and the coastal strip under Ossa and Olympus—by the Mycenaeans led by the royal houses of Orchomenos and Thebes. This will be further considered in Chapter 8 but for the moment it is sufficient to add that at that period Thebes was either an active partner in the Mycenaean confederation or in the later stages absorbed into it after the expedition of the Epigoni, so that since their expulsion the Dorians would have been bitter enemies of the Mycenaeans. It is of course pure speculation but against such a background it is feasible that the tribes known as the

"Myrmidons" who were led by the successors of Achilles would have joined with Dorians led by the Heracleidae—another clan dispossessed by Mycenaeans—in the great invasion by "The Peoples of the Sea" *c* 1192 B.C. The Cadmeians of Thebes, who had been conquered by the Mycenaeans in an earlier stage of this Grecian "Wars of the Roses", would certainly have joined such a movement as soon as the Mycenaean grip on their territory was weakened. According to the Homeric Catalogue Thessaly sent 280 ships to Troy[12] and the Dorians during their residence in Phthiotis and round Ossa and Olympus must have become acquainted with the sea. It is even tempting to equate these people with the Thekel, or one of the other unidentified "Peoples of the Sea" mentioned in the Egyptian records. This would explain the origin of part of the sea power used in this invasion.

The rest of the ships needed for this operation, probably the major part of them, would have been supplied by the sea ports along the eastern Mediterranean coast from Troy southwards, just as centuries later during Alexander's conquests (see the Introduction). These sea ports would have had little difficulty in furnishing an adequate armada for the expedition to Egypt, whether provided willingly by Heracleidae from Rhodes and Lydia, or others who had joined the enterprise, or by naval ports overrun by "The Peoples of the Sea" as they progressed southwards. Byblus alone would have made a substantial contribution, as tablets excavated there record a catalogue of more than a hundred ships.

The archaeological evidence from Rhodes (Chapter 7) shows no indication of marked destruction corresponding to the invasion or to the loss of Troy (*c* 1200 B.C.). So it can be deduced that at this time the Heracleidae in Rhodes changed sides and joined their kinsmen leading the Dorian hosts. Hence the settlements on the island remained undamaged during the passage of "The Peoples" and its culture continued unbroken.

The picture of Achilles is of a man rash and impulsive in action, whereas the Heracleidae, to judge from the traditional decision not to return to the Peloponnese for three generations, were more cautious and could weigh their chances of success before acting. Accordingly, if any weight can be attached to the principles of heredity, we can expect that the Heracleidae would have let the clan of Achilles lead the naval advance guard which met the Egyptians and was defeated. This would offer a plausible explanation for the disappearance of the naval power of Thessaly which had been preponderant at Troy. All this, however, is pure speculation, and in the absence of positive evidence, many other possibilities could be put forward.

REFERENCES

[1] Palmer, L. R., *Mycenaeans and Minoans,* 1961, pp. 164–5.
[2] Hammond, N. G. L., *A History of Greece to 322 B.C.,* 1959, p. 64.
[3] Blegen, C. W., *Troy and the Trojans,* 1963, p. 160.
[4] Hammond, N. G. L., *ibid,* p. 52.
[5] Herodotus, *The Histories,* Penguin Classics, 1963, Book I, p. 80.
[6] Hammond, N. G. L., *ibid,* pp. 51–2.
[7] Hammond, N. G. L., *ibid,* p. 110.
[8] Hammond, N. G. L., *ibid,* pp. 64–5.
[9] Palmer, L. R., *ibid,* p. 84.
[10] Hammond, N. G. L., *ibid,* p. 66.
[11] Hutchinson, R. W., *Prehistoric Crete,* Pelican Books, 1962, p. 317f.
[12] Hammond, N. G. L., *ibid,* p. 65.

CHAPTER SEVEN

The Fall of Troy and After

Now are fields of corn where Troy once was

OVID

SOON after the beginning of the second millennium B.C. a new people penetrated into the Greek peninsula: the so-called "Nordic" race, from somewhere in the north and west of Greece, and possibly originally from the Danube basin. They brought with them the horse and a distinctive pottery known as "Minyan",[1] because it was first found at Orchomenos in the land of the Minyae. Well made on the potter's wheel in distinctive new shapes and with decorations obviously intended to simulate metallic ware, it was distinguished further by its grey colour, resulting from a new technique of firing the vessels under reducing conditions in the kiln. Horse bones and sherds of this pottery mark the trail of this people as they penetrated into Greece.

Apart from the originality and inventiveness portrayed, they were obviously warlike, as these signs of their arrival are found immediately above the burnt-out remains of the earlier settlements they overran. But they do not seem to have been barbaric as in some cases these settlements were not destroyed, and they seem to have mingled rapidly with the existing peoples, who were of the "Mediterranean" race. Skulls from the graves of the period show a blending of broad-headed and long-headed peoples, indicating that the "Nordic" invaders and their "Mediterranean" forerunners had settled down side by side, as the two races can be distinguished by this anatomical detail.

These Nordic "Minyans" seem to have appeared first in Macedonia[2] around 2500 B.C., whence they spread eastwards into Chalcidice and southwards into Thessaly. The prototype of the distinctive Minyan ware had apparently been developed in Macedonia shortly before the end of the Early Bronze Age (before 1900 B.C.), judging from the sherds found there dating from this period. The Minyans' gift for originality was rapidly stimulated by contact with the more developed Mediterranean culture further south. This culture (Chapter 9) had earlier brought to Greece the Neolithic and Bronze Age civilizations of Asia Minor and beyond. By about 1900 B.C. the new people were ready for a further wave of expansion, in which most of the rest of Greece was overrun and Minyan settlements arose, often on the burnt-out ruins of earlier villages, as far south as the Peloponnese.

It appears, therefore, that we can regard the Minyans as the "cement" which held the Greek peoples together. They must have played much the same role in the Aegean as the Normans did in forming the English people. The Greeks, whether Mycenaean, Dorian or the later classical Greeks, must in just the same way be looked upon as a blend of the various peoples who came into the land at various periods. Thus the Greeks ultimately became an ethnical composite of at least the early Neolithic settlers, who probably came from Asia Minor or Syria, with the Early and Middle Bronze Age (or Minyan) peoples from the north, together with other intrusive elements. Naturally the proportion of the different ethnic groups would have varied from area to area, with more Minyans in the north, whilst the earlier stock survived in the south. The Minyans, however, were the common and ultimately dominant factor, contributing amongst other things the essence of the Greek language. This makes understandable Herodotus' definition of his conception of nationality as comprising a common language, common religious beliefs, and common behaviour.

The Dorians from the north and the Mycenaeans from the south therefore must have had a common nationality varying only in the predominance of one ethnic group or the other. We can therefore describe the Dorians as being Mycenaeans, or at least "fringe" Mycenaeans, because by this we understand primarily the culture corresponding to the people known as "Mycenaeans", and the archaeological evidence makes it clear that by the time of the Dorian migrations the Mycenaean culture had spread over Thessaly and into parts of Macedonia. However, both Dorians and Mycenaeans were basically Minyan in derivation. So even the original and early Greek civilization was essentially Aegean in concept and evolution. The early Minyan penetration into northern Greece, followed by the expansion into Asia Minor, ensured this. Therefore the Greeks looked naturally towards the Near Eastern shores of the Aegean and the establishment of the Ionic settlements there, after the Dorian invasions, must have been the continuation of a trend which had commenced with the Minyan incursion into the Troad rather than an innovation.

The Minyans' eastward expansion was a natural step. It is no surprise to learn that Minyan sherds occur in Asia Minor and in Troy especially,[3] dated *c* 1800 BC. The incursion could have taken place by sea or by land through Thrace and across the Hellespont and the Bosporus. If the distribution of Minyan sherds[4] is plotted on a map, two distinct zones of distribution can be seen running in a coastal strip from the Hellespont southwards through Troy towards Miletus, and from the Bosporus in an inland band southwards to Bycesultan. This distribution would favour the land route as the more likely, as we must presume that at that time Troy possessed some naval power since evidence of trading by sea has been revealed by excavations of city levels of pre-Minyan date.

As in the Greek mainland, the Minyans brought to Troy their native culture, developed during their residence in Macedonia, Thessaly and Chalcidice. This[5] included the widespread use of the horse, their distinctive pottery and a number of other features:[6] the small cist grave and the initial use of apsidal dwellings, later developed into rectangular houses which were the prototype of the "Megaron" house of the Mycenaeans centuries later. With the passage of time these included a porch built of wooden pillars, and a circular hearth with a raised platform of consolidated earth apparently used as the base for an oven. The cist graves, however, have not been found in Troy,[7] so presumably the invaders adopted the burial customs they found there. The "Megaron" house in Troy was not an innovation[8] as it had already been in use at least as early as Troy II (*c* 2500–2200 B.C.). It would appear that the development of the Minyan apsidal house into the proto-Megaron type after the arrival of the Minyans in Thessaly must be attributed to the influence of Trojan culture on the Greek mainland rather than the reverse. In view of the evidence for trade between Troy and the Greek mainland and the Cyclades this is not surprising.

Opinion today mostly views the Minyans as the first Greek-speaking peoples to settle on the Greek mainland.[9] Certainly it appears that the first Greeks came from the north as the surviving distribution of place-names of Greek origin[10] is far more pronounced in the north and centre of the peninsula than the south. The most authoritative opinion[11] concludes that the two prongs of Minyan penetration—west into Greece proper—east across the Hellespont and Bosporus—were made up of kinsmen who were branches of the same stock. This leads to the awkward conclusion that both groups must have been Greek-speaking. However, Palmer points out there is no philological evidence surviving,[12] for instance in the place-names in the Troad, to show that Greek was spoken there during this period (Troy VI), which must have covered at least six hundred years from the arrival of the Minyans *c* 1900 B.C.

An adequate explanation can be found for this by comparing the extinction of the Danish language and nationality in those Northmen who settled in Normandy, within two hundred years of its conquest by Duke Rollo. This parallel has been drawn by Hall[13] to explain the extinction of the nationality and language of the Philistines:

> "... The parallel to the extinction of the Danish language and nationality of the Northmen in Normandy two hundred years after Rollo's conquest is curiously exact. So history always repeats itself when conditions are similar."

It is clear that the Minyans, whose northern branch must later be equated with their "Dorian" descendants, were inventive and adaptive, so that their contact with a more advanced culture would have led to the adoption of features superior to their own culture. This may well have happened in Troy, where they would have assimilated Trojan culture and language, whether it was Luvian or a related dialect.

If this is an acceptable explanation, a number of puzzling features become understandable. The Hittite records implying that a Mycenaean mainland king maintained suzerainty over local kingdoms in Asia Minor (Chapter 6) find an explanation in ties of blood and kinship. The old tradition of a Grecian "Thalassocracy" in the Aegean during this period points in the same direction. Palmer[14] has cited from the *Iliad* the example of a grant of land, or *temenos,* to military leaders, in return for feudal service rendered. Sarpedon speaking to his brother-in-arms Glaucos says:[15] "Why have you and I the seats of honour at home, Glaucos? . . . And that fine estate on the banks of Xanthos, orchards and wheatlands of the best? For that, we are bound to stand now before our people in the scorching fires of battle . . ." The puzzle is that both were Lycians and not Mycenaeans. It could be that Homer is attributing to the Trojans and their allies the same customs and organizations that prevailed amongst the Mycenaeans, as recorded in the Pylian tablets; but it is more intelligible if we accept that they were descended from the same Minyan stock who had brought these old Indo-European customs with them from a common source. The same considerations apply, and the same source is indicated, for their common worship of the same gods which Homer repeatedly stresses in his narrative. This will be developed later in relation to Apollo (Chapter 9). The Achaeans and the Trojans emerge as men with similar customs, thinking on similar lines.

Excavations show that although the invaders represented a major break in continuity there is no evidence that the city was destroyed or sacked.[16] The new city they founded (Troy VI) seems to have flourished from about 1800–1300 B.C.,[17] when it was apparently destroyed by a tremendous earthquake. It was rebuilt[18] by the same people, without a break in the continuity of the culture. The fortification walls were rebuilt and extended, probably in haste as the old blocks from the fallen wall were re-used and supplemented by smaller unworked blocks of stone, all of which suggests an emergency. Instead of the rather imposing baronial mansions of the pre-earthquake period we now find within the citadel small houses crowded closely together and separated only by party walls, although some of the great houses were reconstructed and again inhabited. A distinctive feature of the new town (Troy VIIa) was the large storage jars (or *pithoi*) in most houses, sunk into the ground with the rim at floor level, where it was covered with a stone slab. In this way large quantities of foodstuffs, solid and liquid, could be stored without taking up excessive floor space. The normal content of each house ranged from four to a dozen *pithoi*, but in one case as many as twenty were found.[19] The use of *pithoi* for storage had been common practice at Troy and elsewhere, but the normal practice was to stand the vessels either on the floor or in slight depressions used as sockets. We do not find the vessels buried up to their rims at Troy until this period (*c* 1300–1250 B.C.). The citadel was clearly forced to support a much higher density of population than formerly[20] and living space had to be provided without delay. This was no normal expansion, which could have been coped with by extending the citadel walls, or by building houses outside the fortifications.

The inhabitants must have been faced with an emergency where provision had to be made to shelter those who normally resided outside the city: it was of course the opening stage of the "Wars of the Roses" (see also Chapter 6), which became in due course the Trojan War immortalized by Homer. The opening can be dated around the fall of Thebes (*c* 1280 B.C.), and the fall of Troy *c* 1250, taking Blegen's latest date, so that the start of the Trojan War can be fixed around 1260 B.C., or possibly a little earlier, with strained relations and possibly minor hostilities arising in the intervening period.

It has been argued that the remains of Troy VIIa were not consistent with the rich and imposing city of Homer, but the fortification walls and towers tally well with his description. Later, in the Roman and Hellenistic periods, the cap of the mound was shaved off.[21] This removed all remains of structures of Troy VIIa, VIIb and VIII in the centre of the citadel where, as we know, Priam's Palace and the Temple buildings were situated, according to the *Iliad.* Only the remnants of the buildings of Troy VIIa were left in the outer periphery of the acropolis to be uncovered by the archaeologist. Most of what remains today (see Chapter 1, Figure 2) consists of the relics of the dwellings of the poorer people in the periphery of the city. Many were built up against the inner surface of the citadel wall, as in medieval European towns. We cannot compare these refugee quarters with the baronial mansions of earlier times.

Troy VIIa was destroyed by fire, and sacked. Parts of skeletons found in the debris seem to be those of victims killed in the fighting.[22] Blegen dates the life-span of Troy VII from the sherds of Mycenaean pottery found in the ruins, and has no doubt that Troy VIIa can be identified with Homer's city.[23] He places the earthquake *c* 1300, and Troy's destruction by fire *c* 1250 B.C. or even a decade or two earlier. To establish a consistent chronology (Chapter 10) I have taken Blegen's lower date, but a decade either way will not be significant for the interpretation of events.

Archaeological evidence from Thermi in the island of Lesbos shows it was destroyed about the same time as Troy, or a little earlier. This is supported by the story in the *Iliad* of slave women, taken at Lesbos, who were the cause of the breach between Achilles and Agamemnon and who also figured in the gesture of reconciliation made by the latter.

After the capture of Troy the Mycenaeans would certainly have installed a governor, or set up a puppet dynasty. No doubt the Achaean barons and knights who went to Troy would have staked out new kingdoms and dynasties at the expense of Troy's defeated allies. This was the customary reward for military service[24] in the Middle Ages and it can be traced back to the Mycenaeans through the Linear B tablets. That this did happen after Troy fell can be seen from the historical record. As already cited (Chapter 2) the Hittite archives for the period following the sack of Troy (*c* 1250–1190 B.C.) contain a number of references to the king of Achaea and to at least one local Achaean ruler who owed him allegiance. Greek legend also preserved a number of instances where such dynasties were established recording also the names and origin of their founders[25] (Chapter 3).

The chief Trojan allies have been listed in Chapter 6 with the Homeric Catalogues, and as enumerated they stretched from the river Axios in Macedonia as far south as Lycia. The Mycenaeans could therefore expand into a wide arc, southward towards the richer and more sophisticated kingdoms in southern Asia Minor, rather than northward where there would have been more fighting than plunder. The Lycians were the most important ally to the south, and Greek tradition attributed their origin to Crete during the time of Minos—well after the Mycenaean invasion of Crete *c* 1450 B.C.—when there was dynastic trouble and Minos expelled his brother Sarpedon and his party. If this tradition is to be believed, the Lycians had a long-standing enmity with the Mycenaeans so that their active support for the Dorians in the movement of "The Peoples of the Sea" would have been natural. They may have contributed, possibly with Cypriot forces too, to the new nation of the Philistines who kept the coastal regions of the Shephelah after the Egyptian victory.

The new city (Troy VIIb1) arose on the debris of the old and often on the same foundations, and it continued the same unbroken culture. Sherds of the same Grey Minyan and Tan wares, made throughout the lifetime of Troy VI and VIIa, are again found.[26] It is clear that the city was rebuilt by its former inhabitants without delay, though there are indications that the standard of living was lower, as might be expected, for the new masters, while naturally exploiting Troy's strategic position to control the flow of trade, would have ensured that the bulk of the profits were diverted to the homeland. Troy VIIb1 probably endured for about 60 years[27] (from *c* 1250 B.C. to *c* 1195 or 1190 B.C.—see below). It was succeeded by VIIb2, whose strata show that a new type of pottery—"Knobbed Ware"—largely replaced the other types which still prevail in the lower strata.

There is some mystery about the end of Troy VIIb1, as there are no signs of destruction and the fortifications apparently remained undamaged. This indicates that the new masters took over without serious disturbance. The mystery disappears if we accept the theory already discussed in Chapter 3 that "The Peoples of the Sea" were the Dorians, and that they passed through in their drive towards Egypt. The Trojans would have welcomed the invaders, remembering they had been their allies or sympathizers in the Trojan War. The Mycenaeans at Troy could have been in no position to offer resistance, weakened by overexpansion in Asia Minor and Syria and rent by feuds at home as a result of the Trojan War. Probably they evacuated Troy and escaped to the mainland before the full force of the invasion arrived. Hence there are no signs of looting and burning.

The earlier Minyan invasion of Asia Minor was a two-pronged drive. It seems history repeated itself, for "The Peoples of the Sea" probably followed the same routes. The Dorians and their allies would have crossed the Hellespont—a most appropriate name for the crossing which took them, ruled by the "Sons of Hellen", on the long road which in the end led to the conquest of the Peloponnese. The Phrygians, or Muski, would have crossed the Bosporus. The immediate objective of the first drive was the liberation of the Troad, and the target of the second was undoubtedly Hattusas, the capital of the Hittite kingdom, and its wealth. Both the Hittite and the Mycenaean overlords in the Troad must all have been weakened by the conflict which had broken out between them a generation or two earlier (see Chapter 2). This was only the culmination of a continuous sapping of Hittite strength in the long drawn-out struggles with the Egyptians and other states on their southern border, as well as the wild Kaskan tribes in the north, who had apparently even succeeded in sacking the Hittite capital[28] during the reign of Hattusilis III (*c* 1275–1250), presumably when the Hittite army was on a campaign in the south.

The Phrygians may have been distant cousins of the Greeks, as can be seen by comparing the pictorial records available to us: Plate VII shows the "Warrior Vase" found at Mycenae and dated late thirteenth or early twelfth century B.C. The Mycenaean warriors are setting off on an expedition with their "swag-bags" suspended from their spears and the woman on the left is wishing them "god-speed"; Plate VIII is of a Phrygian frieze found in a tomb at Gordia, showing Phrygian warriors. The superficial resemblance is remarkable, although differences of detail are obvious. Whether ties of blood or interest united the Dorians and Phrygians, it seems most likely that the two-pronged attack was concerted. That the Heracleidae planned and led the drive of "The Peoples of the Sea" is supported by the similarity of a two-pronged enveloping attack to that employed a few years later in the conquest of the Peloponnese (Chapter 8). Certainly the attack was successful on both sides; the Troad and the Hittite kingdom were overrun. This must have been about 1195 B.C. to fit with the date of *c* 1192 B.C. for the attempted invasion of Egypt. The date for the liberation of Troy fits well with Blegen's date of *c* 1200 B.C. or a little later for the end of Troy VIIb1 and with the generally-recognized date for the fall of Hattusas (*c* 1200–1190 B.C.).

One interesting discovery, which may be connected with the migration of "The Peoples of the Sea" and may have some bearing on the theory that Rhodes joined with the Dorians in this venture, is that of the wreck of an ancient ship off Cape Gelidonya on the coast of Turkey, about 120 miles east of Rhodes. This wreck, dated *c* 1200 B.C., lies on the direct route from Egypt to Rhodes and the Aegean (see Chapter 4, Reference 8). Its cargo[29] included a large number of copper ingots of the ancient "oxhide" shape, which were recovered deeply incrusted with calcareous deposits so that at first they were mistaken for rocks. These ingots had makers' proofmarks cast into the metal, and inscribed signs scratched on the surface, which may have been the original owners' identification marks. Some ingots had file marks on the edges, interpreted as recording that the metal had been tested for quality.

More than a ton of bronze and copper artifacts was recovered from the wreck, including bronze ploughshares, picks, shovels, axes, including double axe heads, adzes, knives and awls, spear and arrow points and fragments of bronze bowls. Bronze blanks ready to be worked into tools were also found, together with much scrap metal obviously destined for remelting. Some of the tools were inscribed with letters in the Cypro-Minoan script used in Cyprus. Some of the copper ingots were typically Cypriot, whilst others were of a type previously found only in Sardinia. This is puzzling, unless Cyprus produced ingots like those to which the Sardinian market was accustomed. Other artifacts were salvaged including Egyptian scarabs and a fragment of a basket, still in a good state of preservation, made of matting and rope, which from its association had probably held tools, weapons and household articles. The ingenious explanation has been given to account for the nature of this cargo, which also included scales and haematite weights for weighing the metal, that it was that of a travelling smith bound for island or other ports to execute commissions on the spot. However, an alternative explanation is possible.

We have no means of telling positively but it is just possible that this ship—if indeed it sank at the right time—was taking a load of plunder seized by the Dorians from the settlements in Cyprus and destined for Rhodes or the mainland of Greece, where it could have been reshipped or converted into finished weapons for the Dorians. It has been pointed out by Catling[29] that the correspondence of the Cape Gelidonya cargo with metal hoards found in Cyprus is so close that it may be assumed that the ship derived the bulk of its cargo from that island. Also the metal hoards found in the Acropolis at Athens and possibly attributable to a period *after* 1300 B.C., and at Anthedon in Boeotia, dated to the twelfth century B.C., contain material which could have been manufactured in Cyprus. From this the conclusion can be drawn that more fortunate sister ships of the Cape Gelidonya wreck reached Greece in safety.[29] Probably these cargoes also were composed of plunder seized in Cyprus either after the Mycenaean attack of *c* 1221 B.C. or the Dorian raid of *c* 1192 B.C.

The cargo is of course generally consistent with that of a normal trading vessel carrying Cypriot copper and finished or semi-finished bronze and copper articles to the markets served by Cyprus. But tin ingots, converted by the action of the sea into lumps of white powdery oxide, were also salvaged. Tin was not produced in Cyprus; it would have to be imported, so would not be found on an export ship. The same is true to a lesser degree of the export of scrap metal and of bronze articles from the island, particularly if the ship had been carrying a normal trading cargo destined for the Aegean, where the Greeks and Minoans were famous for their bronze products. But the presence of tin ingots, which would have been imported into Cyprus to meet their needs for the production of bronze, and of bronze articles, would fit exactly with what we would expect to find in a ship loaded with plunder seized from Cyprus. The evidence is admittedly very slender, but it is at least an indication.

With the fall of the Hittite empire its accumulated wealth would have become available for the drive towards Egypt, especially as the stocks of the Hittite arsenals included supplies of iron weapons. If any garrison was left behind by the Dorians in the Troad, we must presume that it later rejoined the main body or was absorbed without serious disturbance into the Trojan scene. We are led to this conclusion because of the prevalence of "Knobbed Ware" in the *upper* strata of Troy VIIb in the late subdivision known as VIIb2.[26] The ware was handmade, of crude but strong design; it shows great originality and was long ago recognized as related to similar pottery found in Hungary and dating from the Late Bronze Age. But there is sufficient difference in detail to suggest that[30] the source of the "Knobbed Ware" may be a stage removed from Hungary, and this source may have been Thrace. The ware is not found on the Greek mainland, and so cannot be attributed to the Dorians.

The artifacts of Troy VIIb are consistent with what might be expected after the Dorian invasion. With the Dorian liberation the city did not suffer any marked destruction. But after they had moved on, some wilder tribe from Thrace or its northern boundaries infiltrated into the Troad to fill the vacuum created by the destruction of Mycenaean power and the movement south of the Dorians. These people can well have been allies of Troy in the period covered by the *Iliad,* which describes the Trojan sphere of influence as extending north and west to the Axios. So these latecomers may have been welcomed; there is no sign of destruction,[31] and the miscellaneous artifacts found in Troy VIIb2, which followed their arrival, are generally very similar to those in VIIa and VIIb1. At the same time Grey Minyan and Tan ware continued to be made and sherds are found associated with the new "Knobbed Ware".

The end of ancient Troy came at the close of the twelfth century B.C. or a little later.[32] Archaeology indicates the city was again fired and looted in the chaos that followed the destruction of the Hittite and Mycenaean empires. It was not then rebuilt and remained deserted until the seventh century B.C., when it arose as a Greek colony in which again the Grey Minyan pottery appeared. The original inhabitants must have survived in the area and with more settled times returned to the ancient site.

REFERENCES

[1] Hammond, N. G. L., *A History of Greece to 322 B.C.*, 1959, p. 40f.
[2] Hammond, N. G. L., *ibid*, p. 37.
[3] Blegen, C. W., *Troy and the Trojans*, 1963, p. 140f.
[4] Palmer, L. R., *Mycenaeans and Minoans*, 1961, p. 231.
[5] Blegen, C. W., *ibid*, p. 145.
[6] Hammond, N. G. L., *ibid*, p. 37 and p. 40f.
[7] Blegen, C. W., *ibid*, p. 143.
[8] Blegen, C. W., *ibid*, p. 48.
[9] Blegen, C. W., *ibid*, p. 145.
[10] Hammond, N. G. L., *ibid*, p. 39.
[11] Blegen, C. W., *ibid*, p. 145; Palmer, L. R., *ibid*, p. 227f.
[12] Palmer, L. R., *ibid*, p. 228.
[13] Hall, H. R., *The Ancient History of the Near East*, 1960, p. 72.
[14] Palmer, L. R., *ibid*, p. 95.
[15] Homer, *The Iliad*, Mentor Classics, 1950, p. 146.
[16] Blegen, C. W., *ibid*, p. 110f.
[17] Blegen, C. W., *ibid*, p. 142.
[18] Blegen, C. W., *ibid*, p. 147f.
[19] Blegen, C. W., *ibid*, p. 154f.
[20] Blegen, C. W., *ibid*, p. 156.
[21] Blegen, C. W., *ibid*, p. 150.
[22] Blegen, C. W., *ibid*, p. 160f.
[23] Blegen, C. W., *ibid*, p. 164.
[24] Palmer, L. R., *ibid*, p. 91f.
[25] Herodotus, *The Histories*, Penguin Classics, Book 1, p. 83.
[26] Blegen, C. W., *ibid.*, p. 165f.

[27] Blegen, C. W., *ibid.*, p. 171f.

[28] Gurney, O. R., *The Hittites*, Pelican Books, 1961, p. 37.

[29] Desborough, V. R. d'A., *The Last Mycenaeans and Their Successors*, 1964, p. 49; Throckmorton, P., National Geographic, May 1962, p. 697f; and Catling, H. W., *Cypriot Bronzework in the Mycenaean World*, Clarendon Press, 1964, p. 297f.

[30] Blegen, C. W., *ibid*, p. 169f.

[31] Blegen, C. W., *ibid*, p. 167f.

[32] Blegen, C. W., *ibid*, p. 172.

CHAPTER EIGHT

The Dorian Migrations

When Greeks joined Greeks, then was the tug of war!

LEE

THE Dorians first emerge from the mists of Greek legend in southern Thessaly in the region of Phthiotis. It is, however, most likely that they originally came from the north and were part of that general movement of Indo-European tribes (the Minyans) into Greece which took place in the early part of the second millennium. According to Herodotus[1] they moved northwards from Phthiotis to the land called Histiaotis near the two mountains Ossa and Olympus and including the rich vale of Tempe. This took place between the reigns of Deukalion, traditionally late fourteenth century B.C., and that of king Dorus the son of Hellen and grandson of Deukalion. So the date of this migration, if thirty years make a generation, can be set between 1310 and 1250—say about 1280 B.C. This date coincides with the peak of Mycenaean power, when the kingdoms of Iolkos, Orchomenos and Thebes would have formed part of the Mycenaean confederation. It is consistent with other Mycenaean actions at this time that these kingdoms would have been extending their dominion northwards at the expense of the Dorians, who were likely to have been unruly and warlike neighbours. So the Dorians had a motive for revenge, and this explains their willingness to shelter noble refugees from Thebes, including the Heracleidae, when internal dissensions later broke out in the Mycenaean camp.

According to the tradition preserved by Herodotus, at a later but unknown date the Dorians were again driven out by "Cadmeians", and forced further north and west to Pindus where they became known as Macedonians ("Makednoi"). In the reign of king Dorus, *c* 1250 B.C., Herodotus refers to them living in the region of Ossa and Olympus, so this second eviction must have taken place after that date. Significantly the date we arrive at coincides with Blegen's date for the fall of Troy, so it is tempting to assume that the second migration was forced on the Dorians by the Trojan War.

Around this time, too, or possibly a decade or two earlier, the abortive attempt of Hyllus took place on the Isthmus of Corinth.[2] The two events were probably related, and one might assume that the Dorians' second displacement was forced upon them by the reprisals of the Mycenaeans for the raid of Hyllus. This would have been most likely after the fall of Troy when the returning Mycenaeans were still mobilized and before any serious dissensions had broken out.

So far the customary interpretation of the Greek tradition of the Dorian migrations agrees broadly with this analysis; but from this point on the traditional interpretation is[3] that the Dorians then migrated from Pindus to Dryopis (later known as Doris), between Phocis and Malis, whence they mounted their successful invasion of the Peloponnese, via the northern shore of the Gulf of Corinth, in a sea-borne attack on Corinthia. Customarily the date of this assault is given as *c* 1120 B.C.[4] However, this introduces a dating discrepancy. Archaeology in the case of most of the major Mycenaean centres whose fall is attributed to the Dorians, fixes a date around 1200 B.C. for the fall of Pylos, Mycenae, Tiryns, Thebes, the castle at Gla and other important centres . . . though of course such dating cannot be precise and even under favourable circumstances a margin of fifty years is normal. As developed in Chapter 4 the evidence of the Linear B tablets indicates an invasion from the sea, probably from the south, and there is circumstantial evidence (Chapter 5) that the decisive assault was staged from Asia Minor via Crete. This would appear to discredit the traditional route, while the traditional date of *c* 1120 B.C. appears too low. It may be that different methods have been used for the two datings.

The dates for the destruction of the mainland cities have been based mainly on the Mycenaean pottery in use when the city was sacked, which in turn has been related to the date of other artifacts found in conjunction with such pottery. But the traditional dates for the invasions have been fixed by Greek historians of the classical period on the basis of genealogies and the tradition that the Dorian invasion of the Peloponnese took place two generations after the fall of Troy, while Hyllus' attempt was one generation before the fall. The use of genealogies must be approximate because they are often incomplete, or amended, and the average length of a generation is not fixed. However, we are in a more fortunate position than the Greek historians as we have archaeology to fix certain important dates, such as that of the destruction of Troy VIIa. It cannot be fixed with absolute precision, but I have a slight preference for Blegen's "later" date of *c* 1250.[5] The reasons for this are dealt with in Chapter 7, but as it is about 50 years earlier than the traditional date, it is valuable in reconciling the discrepancy. For if the fall of Troy is put back to 1250, the date for the main Dorian invasions, two generations later, becomes *c* 1190 B.C., taking thirty years to a generation. The actual date is taken as *c* 1195 B.C. to fit the pattern of events elsewhere (see Chapter 10).

After the fall of Troy, Greek legend tells of a split in the Mycenaean confederation, while history and archaeology in Asia Minor indicate a period of overexpansion which spread the Mycenaean power too thin. Their conflict with the Hittites weakened both powers, while the disastrous expedition to Egypt of *c* 1221, as allies of the Libyans, would have strained their resources further. The Egyptian records of the time included the Mycenaeans (or Achaeans) among the chief "Peoples of the Sea", and it is logical to think that the invasion was organized by them.

Within a generation of the fall of Troy, say around 1220 B.C., the Dorians would have reoccupied the region of Ossa and Olympus as a result of the Mycenaean weakness and possibly moved into the Dryopis region too. Therefore, in attempting to identify the Dorians who invaded and destroyed the Mycenaean empire, we do not have to look further than the clans who traditionally occupied these regions—a people who were Mycenaean in their culture and origins, particularly as far as the dominant elements among them were concerned. Mylonas[6] has pointed out that there is no need to look further north and has stressed how unlikely it would have been that invaders from the north would have pressed on further southwards:

> "In a recent visit to Thessaly I was again impressed with the expanse of its fertile ground. Whether you stand at the heights of Pharsala, or those of Kalabaka, or the beginning of the Vale of Tempe you cannot help but be impressed by its arable land. The question comes to mind at once, how could people seeking land to establish themselves have failed to settle there, especially since

the southward advance seems to be barred by a veritable wall of high mountains?"

These rich agricultural areas, which had been the home of the Dorians, were well equipped to furnish the core of the manpower needed for the invasion of "The Peoples of the Sea" and the Dorian conquest of the Peloponnese. Mylonas goes on to emphasize that the Mycenaeans continued to occupy these centres after the mythical barbarians are supposed to have overrun them:[6]

"... our excavations have proved that the Mycenaeans continued to live in their citadel and tend to their walls and storerooms in these walls in the days when LH IIIc ware was being produced. The great amount of that type of ware found recently by Dr. M. Verdelis at Tiryns indicates that the fortress so closely associated with Mycenaean tradition was also fully occupied by Mycenaeans in the early years of the twelfth century B.C., in spite of the categorical statements to the contrary of some scholars."

It is possible, too, that the house of Achilles, who held the northern marches against the Dorians, may have united with the Heracleidae against the central Mycenaean power.

This, in line with the hypothesis of a Greek "Wars of the Roses", could explain the end of Troy VIIb1[7] which (Chapters 7 and 10) has been set at *c* 1195 B.C., the destruction of the Hittite empire of the same date, and the invasion of Egypt *c* 1192 B.C. The Dorians in Macedonia and around Ossa and Olympus, together with the peoples of Thessaly (the "Myrmidons") and the former allies of Troy spread in an arc between the Axios and the Propontis, would have been able to organize and execute these actions. The sea-power needed would have been available—according to Homer Thessaly sent 280 ships to Troy—while the Dorians would have been familiar with the sea, and the sea-power of Rhodes and other Mycenaean centres in the eastern Aegean may well have joined them.

If this is accepted, the Greek traditions of the Dorian invasions fall into line with archaeology. After the initial invasion of Pylos had established a firm bridgehead, their allies would have flooded southward through Boeotia and across the Gulf of Corinth into Corinthia, Achaea and Elis.[8] However, this would have taken place *c* 1192 instead of *c* 1140–1120. This fits well enough with the dates, all around 1200 B.C., established by archaeology for the destruction of all the Mycenaean centres, other than Athens and Eleusis which handed on an unbroken Mycenaean culture. This fits in with Broneer's discovery in 1957 of the remains of a towered fortification wall in the Isthmus of Corinth, dated *c* 1200 by the Mycenaean pottery sherds used in the fill for the foundations.[9] It also explains the Greek tradition[10] that Sparta (Lacedaemonia) held out against the Dorians for several generations, and supports the view that the mountain fastness of Arcadia was barely touched by the Dorians and never conquered, so that it survived into the classical period as a fossil of debased Mycenaean culture. This will be developed further against the philological evidence available.

By updating the Dorian invasions fifty years, we find that many of the previous discrepancies disappear. There remains the part they played in Crete. We learn from the *Odyssey*[11] that at the time of the Trojan War Crete was inhabited by different peoples: the Achaeans, the "great-hearted" Eteo-Cretans, the Kydonians, Pelasgians and Dorians divided into three tribes. Strabo in quoting from the *Odyssey* mentions a note from the historian Staphylos that the Dorians inhabited the eastern part of the island, the Eteo-Cretans centred on their city of Praisos in the south, and the remainder, the most powerful group, occupied the plains, including the rich central Mesara.[12] But by the classical period the *Dorians* were in possession of the Mesara and most of the coastal plains except Kydonia.

This apparent shift calls for an explanation, which can be found in the tradition that the Dorian migration extended to Crete one generation after the foundation of their three kingdoms in the Peloponnese.[12] Their migrations from the north may have taken place almost simultaneously with the invasion of Pylos; but it may well have taken a decade or two before the three kingdoms were *established,* so that we reach a date *c* 1150 for the main invasion of Crete for the purpose of settlement. Before that (Chapter 5), there is evidence that the Dorians had already invaded Crete en route to Pylos, sacking Knossos but only temporarily occupying the Palace. This is likely, for their prime motives would surely have been to plunder Pylos from the Cretan base before the Pylians could mobilize their allies. Also they must have wanted to establish contact with their homeland, which was essential to provide firstly a safe retreat if repulsed by the Pylians and a route for their plunder salvaged from Asia Minor and Crete, and secondly a route for reinforcements to assist in carrying out their plans. It appears that the initial attack on Pylos was successful and the Dorians remained. From that time the coasts of Crete are likely to have been raided frequently for booty and slaves, so it is understandable that the Cretan Palaces remained in ruins and were not fully used again.

The Dorians may have originally settled in the north-eastern and eastern part of Crete as immigrants from the Dodecanese islands,[13] or they may even have arrived from Asia Minor (Chapter 9). It is more likely that they came or were reinforced *c* 1450 B.C. when the main Mycenaean invasion of Crete took place after the volcanic eruption of Thera. This would explain at least some of the early Dorian settlements. About a century after the Mycenaean invasion the Dorians were in Phthiotis. Part of the Mycenaean navy may have been destroyed by the same tidal waves which swept the Cretan coasts, so they would have looked elsewhere for reinforcements to Pylos, Thessaly and the northern mainland coast. So the Dorians may have been rewarded for this participation by the gift of feudal dependencies in the north-east of the island, whilst the Mycenaeans retained the rich coastal and central plains. This possibility would have been strengthened if there had been earlier Dorian settlements in the east of the island, which was the case, as mentioned by Staphylos, two centuries later (*c* 1250 B.C.). In these circumstances it would have been natural that after the invasion of Crete (*c* 1450 B.C.) the Dorian part of the Mycenaean influx would join their own kinsmen there and help to hold that part of the island in fief to the Mycenaean overlords at Knossos. This would also fit in with Hutchinson's observation[14] that in the east of Crete there is more archaeological evidence of building and prosperity after the Mycenaean conquest (*c* 1450 B.C.) and yet there is no evidence of Achaean settlements there; he attributes this to the Eteo-Cretans—with whom on Staphylos' evidence we must also group the Dorians—who acted as "quislings" in the east in order to escape the heavy hand of "Minoan Mallia".

We now return to the main Dorian invasion of Crete about 1150. The conquerors would have seized the coast and central plains and driven the Mycenaeans into less accessible or desirable parts with many of their Cretan subjects. Archaeology indicates that the Dorians never seized complete control, unlike the Mycenaeans who, on the evidence of the Linear B tablets from Knossos, were overlords of the whole island. In the classical period the Dorians controlled the Mesara and the coastal plains except Kydonia,[15] so that apparently they were content with the most valuable part only. The Mycenaeans eked out a precarious existence in "Cities of Refuge" (see Chapter 5).

According to tradition, the Dorians took over Cythera and Thera, as well as Crete and other islands, in the generation succeeding the occupation of the Peloponnese, in the time of Eurysthenes and Procles, the sons of Aristodemus, one of the Heracleidae.[10] This would have been *c* 1160, around the same time as the Dorian occupation of Crete, or a little earlier. Huxley[16] has recalled that Herodotus quotes a genealogy for Aigeus, attributing his descent to Theras, one of the leaders of the Dorians, who left Sparta with a band of followers for the island which subsequently took his name, and records that some of them were Minyans who had come to Laconia from Lemnos at the time of the Dorian arrival in Sparta. Pindar also stated that the family of Aigeus had ties with Thebes. All this is very interesting as it links recruits to the Dorian incursions into the Peloponnese with the coasts of Asia Minor, in the neighbourhood of Troy, and again we find the pattern Dorians—Coasts of Asia Minor—Thebes. This piece of information about uninvited reinforcements from the coasts of Asia Minor makes sense when it is realized that the invading Dorians had passed through there.

There is a Greek tradition[17] preserved by Herodotus that the Phoenicians expanded into the Greek islands and occupied Thera, presumably with at least a trading-post, for eight generations, of which three were after the Trojan War. If they were expelled by the Dorians, this would again indicate a date of *c* 1160 for the invasion of Thera. Legends preserve many of the sources, mainly from the Peloponnese, from which the conquerors came, and the Dorian influence extended to the coasts of Asia Minor, notably Cnidus and Halicarnassus.

We may now consider whether the theory (Chapter 3) that the initial invasion of the Peloponnese was via Asia Minor, is supported by the philological evidence. Palmer and others have presented a clear picture of the linguistic background in classical times. The distribution of the

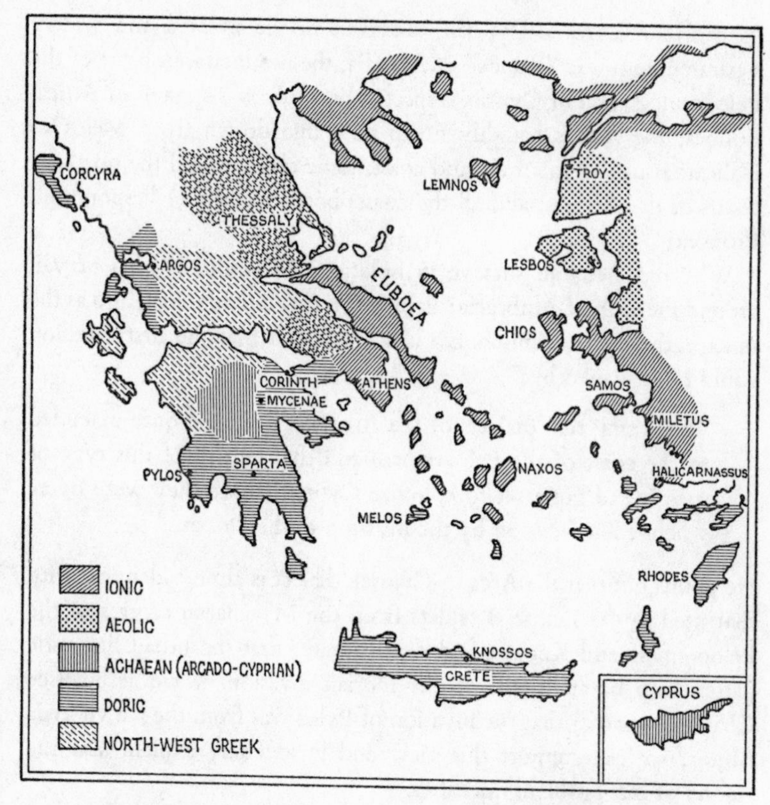

Figure 5. The Distribution of the Greek Dialects in Classical Times

Greek dialects (Figure 5) contains at first sight some puzzling features. The general pattern shows the Dorian dialect prevalent in the south and east of the peninsula, including Tiryns, Mycenae and Corinth, in Crete and in the chain of islands, including Rhodes, linking it to the mainland, and on the coast of Asia Minor itself. The Doric dialect stopped short of Attica, which successfully resisted the Dorian invasions. The north-west Greek dialect was closely linked with the Dorian dialect and covered the islands of Kephallenia, Ithaca, Zacynthos, Elis and Achaea in the Peloponnese, Aetolia, Doris and Phocis to the north of the Gulf of Corinth, and was blended with the Aeolic dialect in Thessaly and Boeotia. Apart from the last two areas, Aeolic was spoken in the islands round Lesbos and the coasts of Asia Minor. Achaean

(Arcadian or Arcado-Cyprian) survived in the isolated and widely separated linguistic "islands" of Arcadia, the mountainous heart of the Peloponnese, and of Cyprus respectively. Ionic was spoken in Attica, Euboea, the islands roughly north of a line drawn from Melos to Halicarnassus and the mainland coast. Ionic also covered the northern coasts of the Aegean, and all the coasts bordering the Hellespont and Propontis.

Why did Achaean survive in isolation? Why did Dorian prevail around the Gulf of Ambracia? Palmer[18] recalled that as long ago as the nineteenth century philologists had concluded that the first question could be answered by:

> "supposing that dialects of the Arcadian type had once extended to the coast of the Peloponnese and that Greeks of this type of speech had gone off to colonize Cyprus before they were overwhelmed and cut off by the invasion of the Dorians."

He points out that the Arcado-Cyprian dialect is almost identical with that used in the Linear B tablets from the Mycenaean centres of the Peloponnese and Knossos and demonstrates that the broad linguistic pattern can be attributed to the Dorian invasion. If we accept (see Chapters 3 and 4) that the invasion of Pylos was from the sea via Asia Minor, we can support this view and incidentally explain also the second of our problem questions.

The Arcadian pocket of Achaean dialect is consistent with a seaborne invasion from the south, as the defeated Pylians and other Achaeans, cut off from escape to the east, would have fled to the central mountain fastness. This situation could not have arisen if the *initial* invasion had come from the north, for the Dorians, themselves tough hillmen, would not have left behind a large isolated pocket of Achaeans as they proceeded from their traditional landing in Corinthia[19] into the Peloponnese. To do so would have exposed their flank and a long line of communications. Also they were assaulting a warlike confederation of kingdoms whose strength lay in chariotry, and therefore to make a long march round the coastal periphery would have been to invite disaster. I believe that the Dorians would first have infiltrated through the mountainous regions of Arcadia had they in fact come from the north, and then would have debouched on the plains with their communications and line of retreat assured. The Mycenaeans would surely have fallen back under such an onslaught, first along the land route to Athens, until it was cut, and then possibly by sea to such allies as Crete, with Athens as the ultimate focus for resistance. But if the attack was from the south initially, with an immediately subsequent one from the north by their kinsmen, the Dorian pattern becomes clear. The Pylians retreated into the Achaean uplands of Arcadia and were trapped there when the attack overran the main Mycenaean cities and cut off the direct escape to Athens.

The Dorians would first of all have been occupied in subjugating and sharing out the rich Mycenaean cities and lands, and later in seizing the overseas dependencies such as Crete, and in subjugating Sparta so as to unite their newly-won domains in Pylos and the Argolid. With such rich prizes it is not surprising that they did not at first undertake the conquest of Arcadia. The delay gave that area time to consolidate its resistance and later the undertaking was not worthwhile.

The Cyprus "island" of Achaean dialect could be explained as Palmer develops[20]—that it had been cut off by the Dorian invasion when it progressed south-eastward through the islands. But if we take this traditional view, why did Cyprus survive the Dorian onslaught? It was a valuable prize as the chief supplier of copper to the ancient world. The Dorians would not have fully penetrated to this area until after the *traditional* date of *c* 1120 B.C. for the occupation of Thera[10] and somewhat later for that of Crete. This date falls right in the period of decadence of the Egyptian state during the time of the Ramessides (*c* 1172–1100 B.C.) starting with Ramesses IV, and the same would be true if the traditional dates for the Dorian occupation of these islands were updated to about 1150.

Had they come at this time, the Dorians would have concentrated on seizing Cyprus, and the Egyptians would have been too weak to resist them. But if the main drive through the islands was westerly, at an earlier date, starting from Asia Minor and Syria after the defeat by Ramesses III, they would certainly not have been able to hold Cyprus as it was within the sphere of Egyptian interests and Ramesses III was strong enough to protect it. Indeed at the time of the attack by "The Peoples of the Sea" it is likely that the Mycenaeans in Cyprus were allies of the Egyptians and would have supplied part of the naval power used by Ramesses III to repel the incursion.

Excavations at Enkomi in Cyprus show that the Mycenaeans took over about the time Crete fell to them, about 1450.[21] There are signs that Enkomi was destroyed again in the late thirteenth century and this has been attributed to "The Peoples of the Sea".[22] But the site revived and the artifacts from its reoccupation are sub-Mycenaean. Tradition claims that after the fall of Troy the Mycenaeans took over many kingdoms, founding new dynasties[23] in Cyprus at Curium, Lapathus, Paphus, Salamis and Soli and the record specifies the areas where these noble families originated (Chapter 7). So archaeology and traditions agree.

The Dorians certainly landed in Cyprus, but they would have had to evacuate it hurriedly after their defeat by the Egyptians. I think that the flourishing town of Enkomi V[24] is to be attributed to Mycenaean founding after the Trojan War. Its destruction shortly after would be due to the invasion by "The Peoples". The new site of Enkomi IV remained Mycenaean. Such an outline explains the survival of the Achaean dialect in Cyprus.

Why did an "island" of Dorian dialect persist around the Gulf of Ambracia? Tradition[25] claims that the north-west Greeks, coming in particular from Aetolia under the leadership of Oxylus, invaded the north-west of the Peloponnese; while the Dorians invaded Corinthia and from there occupied the south and west of the peninsula. This is quite out of line with the isolation of Dorian as an "island", but the problem is explained if we accept that the Dorians invaded the Peloponnese from the south-east. The Gulf of Ambracia gave a direct route northwards through the river valley and Dodona to the Pindus region, giving them their essential link homewards. So, in the initial impetus after the fall of Pylos, they would have driven northwards along the west coast to ensure this line of communication and to seize Corcyra, worth taking for itself and for the control it gave over the "amber" route northwards through the Adriatic and to Italy. But the islands of Ithaca, Kephallenia and Zacynthos were not essential for this purpose, so that the Dorians could allow them to fall to their north-west Greek allies. This seems more probable than that the Dorians "leapfrogged" over the north-west Greeks to dispossess them of this northern part of their territory.

There is an alternative suggestion that this pocket of Dorian dialect can be attributed to the foundation of colonies in these areas by Corinth around the seventh century B.C., but as the philologists estimate that Doric was spoken here by classical times, I do not see why the Gulf of Ambracia should have been an exception to the pattern of colonies established by Corinth, all the rest of which continued to speak the north-west Greek tongue.

For the Heracleidae and their Dorian henchmen, the Peloponnese would have been the promised land, and once there they would have drawn upon their manpower from the Pindus area and from Ossa and Olympus. They would have left the balance of power in Thessaly, Boeotia and Macedonia for their north-west Greek allies, a natural result as the original Mycenaeans there spoke the Aeolic dialect.[26] If it is correct that the house of Achilles threw in its lot with the Heracleidae and the Dorians after the Trojan War, then it is understandable that the remaining Mycenaeans and the north-west Greek peoples should have blended and Thessaly and Boeotia should have developed a blend of the Doric and Aeolic dialects. In Boeotia and the other areas speaking the north-west Greek dialect, the population was not reduced to serfdom,[27] a marked contrast with the behaviour of the conquerors elsewhere, notably in the Peloponnese (with the exception of Arcadia), where the indigenous peoples found them hard masters. The preferential treatment is explained if the penetration of the north-west Greeks into Thessaly and Boeotia was a "take-over" or *Anschluss* with their allies.

These mass movements to the south would have left at least a partial vacuum in the harsher regions left behind. Tribes or nations at this period were relatively small, and the acquisition of richer lands would have brought most of the population to them. The wilder tribes to the north and west, perhaps even allies or mercenaries for the Dorians and north-west Greeks, would have occupied the areas vacated, perhaps peacefully, but it is more likely that the less warlike of those remaining may ultimately have been overrun by force. The successive migrations of the Dorians, from Phthiotis to the final overrunning of the Peloponnese, are set out in Figure 6 (back endpapers), which shows the routes and an indication of the dates.

The Ionic dialect survived in Attica and Euboea, where the invaders were resisted. The so-called "Homeric" hymns written for the priests of Delphi (Chapter 5) seem to make two references to the Dorian invasion. As well as connecting the assault with Crete, they also refer to the traditional route followed, elaborating on the conventional route from the north by specifically mentioning Iolkos and Euboea. They mention that the passage then went across the narrows to the mainland. However, in classical times the dialect in Euboea was Ionic not Doric or north-west Greek, so that we can infer that the Mycenaean resistance, spearheaded by Athens, succeeded in recovering Euboea, no doubt partly because once the Dorians and their allies had consolidated their hold on the mainland, the possession of Euboea was no longer vital for their communications.

The survival of Athens is supported by tradition and archaeology. Oscar Broneer made a great contribution to our knowledge of Athens at this period[28] in his work on the northern slope of the Acropolis in the 1930s, when he unearthed the remains of an entrance gate, defended by a tower, with a stairway leading down from it. The pottery associated with these structures was from the late Mycenaean IIIb period (*c* 1300–1225 B.C.) and showed that this path was abandoned before the end of the period, as houses had been built over it. However, these had been hurriedly evacuated, with rough household pottery left scattered over the floors, but with no indication of fire. The pottery shows no break in style, so it would seem that the invaders did not succeed in overwhelming Athens.

The interpretation of these finds must be that Athens prudently strengthened her defences in the troubled times following the Trojan War. As a result, being well placed geographically, and not involved in the power struggle—unlike the other Mycenaean kingdoms—she grew and prospered. So the "common man" built houses close to the shelter of the citadel walls, though later the threat of the Dorian invasion caused these to be hastily abandoned, and perhaps they were levelled to restore the "field of fire" from the walls. Another discovery of Broneer's, made a decade later, when probing further in a known underground passage to the west of the Erechtheum, uncovered a stairway leading down through a fissure in the rock to a wellspring. This was reminiscent of the similar subterranean water-supplies protected by the citadel walls at Mycenae and Tiryns. The Athens stairway was built of wood so that it could be replaced and repaired when unsettled conditions demanded a protected water-supply. Clearly these did not last long enough to make a more permanent staircase necessary, so that it is unlikely to have been used for more than a generation or two. The associated pottery remains all belong to the late Mycenaean IIIc period, starting about 1225 B.C. This dating agrees well with the Dorian invasion of Pylos, given by Blegen as about 1200 and taken by us (Chapter 4) as around 1192.

The rest of the linguistic pattern conforms to the tradition of the Aeolian and Ionian migrations, with which we are less immediately concerned. The Aeolic colonies were established on the islands and coasts of Asia Minor south of Troy and centred on Lesbos. The colonists, apparently led by the Penthilidae, presumably represented those Aeolians opposed to union with the north-west Greeks. The Ionian colonies and dialect covered the islands and Asia Minor coast east of Athens, bounded approximately by the northern fringe of the Dorian settlements and on the north by the Aeolic colonies. Later they extended further, north of the band of Aeolian colonies, to new settlements whose value was their control of the trade routes into the Black Sea, northwards into the basin of the Danube and beyond, and eastwards along the Meander river into Asia Minor and more distant lands.

The dates of the Aeolic and Ionic migrations would be traditionally placed *c* 1140 and *c* 1020 B.C. if the fall of Troy took place about 1200 and if Neleus, the leader of the Ionic movement, lived in the sixth generation afterward, while the Aeolic migration took place four generations earlier.[29] But if the fall of Troy was *c* 1250, we arrive at dates of *c* 1190 and *c* 1070 respectively. The resurgence of Miletus took place in the first half of the eleventh century B.C.,[30] which fits well with this latter date, while the Ionic migration responsible would have followed from the influx of Mycenaean refugees into Attica after the final "Granary" destruction at Mycenae (*c* 1150 or 1130). Moreover, action in the eastern Aegean by the Attic Mycenaeans at this time was more or less forced upon them by the Aeolic and Dorian expansions which threatened from the north and south to encroach upon the remaining Mycenaean sphere of influence in the central Aegean islands.

At the end of the great migrations the Dorians possessed most of the richest areas in the Greek mainland and islands, and so controlled the approaches to Syria, Egypt and Mesopotamia. All this had been accomplished at the expense of the Mycenaean kingdoms, on whom the Heracleidae and their Dorian followers had been more than amply revenged. There followed a period of exhaustion and consolidation, but the ancient hatreds and rivalries remained between the new Dorian kingdoms and Athens, the last centre of Mycenaean power. Thus the stage was set for events which culminated in the Peloponnesian Wars (*c* 466–404 B.C.), but that lies far outside our present sphere.

REFERENCES

[1] Hammond, N. G. L., *A History of Greece to 322 B.C.*, 1959, p. 59; Herodotus, *The Histories,* The Penguin Classics, 1963, Book I, p. 33.

[2] Herodotus, *ibid,* Book 9, p. 561.

[3] Hutchinson, R. W., *Prehistoric Crete,* Pelican Books, 1962, p. 317.

[4] Hammond, N. G. L., *ibid,* p. 75.

[5] Blegen, C. W., *Troy and the Trojans,* 1963, p. 160.

[6] Mylonas, G. E., *Priam's Troy and the Date of its Fall,* Hesperia, 33 (1964), pp. 378n and 380.

[7] Blegen, C. W., *ibid,* p. 172.

[8] Hammond, N. G. L., *ibid,* p. 75.

[9] MacKendrick, P., *The Greek Stones Speak,* 1962, p. 125.

[10] Hammond, N. G. L., *ibid,* p. 78.

[11] Homer, *The Odyssey,* The Penguin Classics, Book XIX, p. 249.

[12] Hutchinson, R. W., *ibid,* p. 318.

[13] Hutchinson, R. W., *ibid,* p. 319.

[14] Hutchinson, R. W., *ibid,* p. 299.

[15] Hutchinson, R. W., *ibid,* p. 319.

[16] Huxley, G. L., *Early Sparta,* 1962, p. 23.

[17] Hammond, N. G. L., *ibid,* p. 58.

[18] Palmer, L. R., *Mycenaeans and Minoans,* 1961, p. 144.

[19] Hammond, N. G. L., *ibid,* p. 75f.

[20] Palmer, L. R., *ibid,* p. 144f.

[21] MacKendrick, P., *ibid,* p. 132.

[22] MacKendrick, P., *ibid,* p. 133.

[23] Hammond, N. G. L., *ibid,* p. 73.

[24] Desborough, V. R. d'A., *The Last Mycenaeans and Their Successors,* p. 23.

[25] Hammond, N. G. L., *ibid,* p. 79.

[26] Palmer, L. R., *ibid,* p. 145f.

[27] Hammond, N. G. L., *ibid,* p. 81f.

[28] MacKendrick, P., *ibid,* p. 120.

[29] Hammond, N. G. L., *ibid,* p. 84.

[30] Desborough, V. R. d'A., *ibid,* p. 254.

CHAPTER NINE

Cross Fertilization

There is always something new from Africa

PLINY

THE influence of foreign cultures on the Greek mainland and islands has long been recognized; Evans emphasized Egypt's influence on the earlier Cretan civilization in the Mesara and elsewhere, and the dominant role later of Minoan culture and political power in Greece. The first settlers[1] on the Cycladic islands and Greek mainland (*c* 3000 B.C.) are believed to have come from Asia Minor or Syria, as are later waves of immigrants who came to the Cyclades and central and eastern Crete during the early Bronze Age (*c* 2600–2000 B.C.). In the eighth century B.C. the influence of Asia Minor and the Near East led to the Cretan Orientalizing period and then spread to the Dorian mainland centres of Corinth and Sparta and somewhat later to Attica and Ionia.[2] The origin of the art of writing in Greece is attributed to the same source. Most recent authorities recognize that the earlier form of writing in Crete, Linear A, originated thus[3] and the only question is on which language it is based, whether Luvian or another.[4]

The reciprocal effect of Grecian culture on other areas has also been recognized. Evans accepted the influence of Mycenaean culture on Minoan during his later "decadent" Palace period (*c* 1450–1400 B.C.); Cyrus H. Gordon has pointed out the common background to Greek and Hebrew civilization;[5] and many other examples include Minoan and Mycenaean pottery exports to Egypt and the use of Cretan artists to paint frescoes on the palace floors[6] of XVIIIth Dynasty Pharaohs (*c* 1580–1320 B.C.). In ceramics, the reciprocal influence of the Grecian and Minoan styles of mainland pottery is clear. For instance, in Cyprus before 1450 B.C.,[7] when the Mycenaeans dominated Knossos and its possessions, the pottery style at Enkomi had been entirely Cypriot. After that date Mycenaean pottery begins to be found. Near the end of the LH IIIb period Enkomi, and other cities in Cyprus, were destroyed; the new city which arose on its ruins contained fine ashlar masonry, reminiscent of Mycenaean work; and as well as local Cypriot ware we find early LH IIIc pottery.[8]

This Mycenaean style resembles that of Argos at this time, and clearly it was brought to Cyprus—presumably after the earlier of the attacks on Egypt by "The Peoples of the Sea"—by the Mycenaean conquerors who, as mentioned in Chapter 8, expanded into this region after the conquest of Troy about 1250 B.C. and set up new dynasties, seizing Enkomi amongst other places, and by others who followed them to Cyprus as refugees from the Dorians. This fits well with the Egyptian record that the Achaeans (Mycenaeans) participated in the Libyan attack by sea on Egypt about 1221 B.C., as the Mycenaeans would have found Cyprus an ideal advance base for mounting their naval attack.

The second serious destruction of the main sites in Cyprus[9] can, I think, be attributed to "The Peoples of the Sea" about 1192 B.C. The bulk of the pottery from Sinda at this time was LH IIIc1b in type (*c* 1200–1130 B.C.) which shows close connections with Argive LH IIIc pottery.[10] After this second attack on Egypt the "local" Mycenaeans, and perhaps refugees from Cyprus, expanded south into Palestine to form the Philistine kingdom, becoming identified as "Pelasgians".[11] Certainly a pottery type known as "Philistine Ware" appeared on the mainland around this time, which Desborough dates *c* 1165 B.C. or earlier. It is almost identical with the Cypriot material resembling the Mycenaean style from Argos.[12] Enkomi was once more rebuilt and the pottery sherds from the remains of the new settlement are sub-Mycenaean, again showing the reciprocal influence of the Greek mainland, and suggesting sea communication with Cyprus.

Still later (*c* 1190–1070 B.C.), as outlined in Chapter 8, the Aeolic and Ionic migrations brought to the mainland of Asia Minor their native cultures, which subsequently came into full flower in the Ionic period.

It is clear that more weight must be given to the Greek traditions of the early Thalassocracies, including that of Minos, king of Crete, and that the trade and influence of the Minoans and Mycenaeans were more widespread than has been generally recognized. They were the means of reciprocal influence on Asia Minor and Syria. On the basis of this thesis of "cross fertilization", it would be of interest to trace further evidence by archaeology and the historical record. We may first assume that, if such close contact existed, a local disturbance would have had detectable consequences elsewhere; if an area was overrun or subjugated by invasion, military, commercial and artistic interests would emigrate where there were already close relations, taking with them their wealth, experience and expertise. Such a massive influx would have detectably influenced the host culture. On the other hand, there would be at least a partial tendency to return home when settled conditions had returned.

Marked parallels are therefore apparent between the dates of important political events in one area and their cultural and political effects elsewhere, particularly in Greece, Crete and Anatolia/Syria. The most important of these are given below in chronological order:

c 2000 B.C. Events: The conquest of northern Syria by the XIIth Dynasty Egyptian Pharaohs (*c.* 2000–1900 B.C.) Sesostris I and Sesostris II.[13] Possibly the somewhat mythical exploits of the Akkad Dynasty[14] (*c* 2350–2150 B.C.) which were claimed to extend to the Mediterranean may also have been an influence. Excavations in the area of the Egyptian conquests show vividly the ruthlessness of such conquests and precautionary emigration from the rich trading cities in their path is understandable.

Consequences: The middle Minoan period commenced in Crete *c* 2000 B.C. and the first palace at Knossos was built about 1950.[15] The first palaces at Mallia and at Phaistos can be dated respectively *c* 1900–1850 B.C. and *c* 1900 B.C.[16] It is no coincidence that the Cretan hieroglyphic script originated at the start of this period, and its mainland affinities are generally recognized.

c 1800–1700 B.C. Events: The Hittites under King Anittas seized the greater part of the Cappadocian plateau,[17] and then expanded south and west, destroying the Assyrian trading colony or "karum" at Kültepe (Kanesh) and the Arzawan palace at Bycesultan (all about 1800).

Consequences: The palace at Knossos was completely remodelled in the second middle Minoan period (*c* 1850–1750). Much of this news building must have been in the period *c* 1800–1750, to which Evan had assigned the fresco of the "Saffron Gatherer", though it may be later, while the Knossos "Town Mosaic", giving a good idea of the general appearance of Minoan town dwellings, can be similarly dated.[18]

The palaces of Mallia and Phaistos were both reconstructed in the middle Minoan IIIa period, apparently after a severe earthquake about 1730 B.C.[19]

Leonard Woolley has drawn attention to the unmistakable resemblance in building methods and architecture between Yarim-Lim's palace at Atchana, in the ancient kingdom of Yamkhad,[20] and Knossos:

> "There can be no doubt but that Crete owes the best of its architecture, and its frescoes, to the Asiatic mainland";

and he rightly emphasizes here the influence of trade and the emigration of technical experts. Hutchinson[21] records the similarity of the miniature frescoes at Knossos to those in the palace of King Zimri-Lim (*c* 1790–1760 B.C.) at Mari on the Upper Euphrates (captured by Hammurabi of Babylon about 1760 B.C.). As the latter seem more than a hundred years earlier than those at Knossos, they presumably influenced the Cretan murals rather than *vice versa.* Mellaart's recent discovery of coloured wall-paintings about 9000 years old[22] at Çatal Hüyük, about 40 miles from Konya in the Anatolian plain, strongly suggests that this form of decoration originated in Anatolia.

c 1650–1590 B.C. Events: The Hittite kings Hattusilis I (*c* 1650–1620 B.C.) and again Mursilis I (*c* 1620–1590 B.C.) seized Aleppo in Yamkhad,[23] the latter apparently destroying it after a revolt about 1595 B.C.

Consequences: The rise of Mycenae begins, as is evidenced by the rich Grave Circle B (*c* 1650–1550 B.C.)[24] and Grave Circle A (*c* 1580–1500 B.C.),[25] in which latter period perhaps the earliest primitive palace was built on the top of the citadel hill.[24]

c 1450 B.C. Events: Conquest of Crete by the Mycenaeans about this date.

Consequences: Aegean potsherds, found in Akhenaten's (*c* 1380–1365 B.C.) palace at Tell-el-Amarna,[26] must be dated to the third late, Minoan/Mycenaean period, indicating that Cretan artisans found refuge in Egypt. This also holds true for frescoes of Aegean type found in XVIIIth Dynasty palaces, already mentioned. In the late Minoan Ib period, around the time of Pharaoh Thothmes III (*c* 1460), the majority of Aegean pots in Egypt were of Mycenaean rather than Minoan type, so that the fifteenth century B.C. is the period during which the mainland traders began to replace Cretans in the Egyptian and Near East markets.[27]

c 1370–1300 B.C. Events: *c* 1370, and again *c* 1340, the Hittites under King Suppiluliumas seized Aleppo and Atchana and overran Syria from the Euphrates to the sea.[28] The kingdom of Kizzuwatna was involved in the war.[29]

Consequences: In Mycenae the early Cyclopean walls (*c* 1350), the Pillar Room, the south-west wing, the Court and Megaron of the Palace were constructed.[30]

There was also ambitious construction at Tiryns, of which Phase I must be dated *c* 1370 and Phase II *c* 1320 B.C.[31]

The Palace at Pylos was apparently built about 1300.

c 1250–1200 B.C. Events: The Mycenaean confederation conquered Troy and expanded into Asia Minor and Syria at the expense of Troy's allies.

Consequences: Mycenaean settlements and artifacts appeared[32] as far south as al Mina/Sabouni, in the Amq plain on the Syrian coast near Antioch, which must be identified with the Poseidium of the later Greek writers.[33]

It must not be imagined that this "cross fertilization" was the sole cause of the "upsurges" in Aegean civilization, but it was the *contribution* of wealth and knowledge from elsewhere which improved the local culture. The handicap in early times of lack of wealth to the economy and political development was clearly recognized by Thucydides.[34] Homer described Mycenae as "rich in gold"—very aptly, as the marvellous finds by Schliemann and others of worked gold in the graves have shown. Apart from the gains of trade and piracy, at least part of the Mycenaean gold may have come from Egypt, where Nubia was an outstanding source, as payment for mercenaries or rewards for valour when serving in the Egyptian forces, particularly as the Egyptian records show that an award of gold was customary for outstanding military service. Now the Greek traditions contain references to the founding of dynasties in the second millennium B.C. by kings from outside the Mycenaean territories, notably Asia Minor, Phoenicia and Egypt. I would suggest that at least some of these founders may have been not foreigners but Greek leaders of condottieri returning from Egypt, or merchant princes returning from Asia Minor or Syria after one of the political crises mentioned above. It was customary for the younger sons of Indo-European noble families to seek their fortunes in such a way, right up to the feudal Middle Ages, while trade and piracy were not clearly separated in ancient times.

Such leaders would have returned home with bodyguards, wealth, a retinue of technical experts, and concomitant knowledge and prestige. They would have been able to set up new dynasties by marriage, conquest or feudal service to the mainland powers, and although true foreigners cannot be ruled out, this would have been far easier for a returning Greek. It is indicative that such new dynasties do not seem to have introduced foreign peoples into Greece but became hellenized themselves.

Taking the traditional dates for such dynasties[35] and adjusting them to Blegen's latest date—*c* 1250 B.C.—for the fall of Troy (see Chapter 10), we obtain the following results:

Date of Foundation	*Place of Foundation*	*Name of Founder*	*Origin*
c 1520 B.C.	Argos	Epaphus	from Egypt
c 1430 B.C.	Thebes	Cadmus	from Phoenicia
c 1430 B.C.	Orchomenos	Minyas	from Thessaly
c 1370 B.C.	Corinth	Sisyphus	from Thessaly
c 1330 B.C.	Pylos	Neleus	from Thessaly
c 1310 B.C.	(Mycenae)	Pelops	from Asia

The number of dynasties founded from Thessaly, and their situation, immediately attracts attention. There is also the coincidence that two dynasties were founded *c* 1430 B.C., both dominating the Boeotian plain. These traditions may be linked with the Mycenaean invasion of Crete about 1450 (Chapter 5), which may well have been led by the ruling member of the house of Epaphus. Epaphus' date (*c* 1520 B.C.) falls within the period when the Grave Circle A was constructed at Mycenae, and he could well have been one of the hypothetical younger sons who had served in Egypt. There was evidently an interesting story about the advent of Epaphus to the Peloponnese; it is referred to by Herodotus,[36] but unfortunately he did not repeat it as it "has been chronicled by other writers".

Epaphus' descendants would have maintained their Near Eastern contacts, and would have known of the vulnerability of Crete's riches, once the island's northern shore was devastated by a tidal wave. They would have appreciated the value of sea power from their knowledge of the Byblos sea trade with Egypt and the Phoenician trader pirates, and they would have turned to Phoenicia and Thessaly for the extra ships needed to invade Crete.

The date of about 1430 B.C. for the foundation of the dynasties at Orchomenos and Thebes coincides, within the error of determination, with the estimated date of this invasion. The Mycenaeans, as a reward for their allies, may have found it an act of sound statesmanship to give them not only a share in the plunder, but also these two kingdoms, establishing them with almost Machiavellian foresight side by side in the Boeotian plain, to act as a mutual check. The allocations were sound (with Orchomenos awarded to Minyas from Thessaly, contiguous with his homeland; and Cadmus from Phoenicia sandwiched between Orchomenos and the Mycenaean kingdoms to the south) and well-justified, as about 1280 B.C. we find Thebes hostile to the Mycenaean confederation, and attacked by the expedition of the Epigoni. The Mycenaeans in Thessaly, centred on Iolkos,[37] must have been important in the confederation, holding Thebes in check, and together with Orchomenos, controlling the northern marches much as the Percy family did in England during the Middle Ages. They would have had the task of pushing the Dorians northwards and westwards at the time of the Dorian king Dorus (*c* 1280 B.C.), as developed in Chapter 8.

This northern Mycenaean kingdom appears to have stayed faithful to its overlords during the two centuries after the conquest of Crete, and members of the ruling house were apparently rewarded with Corinth (*c* 1370 B.C.) and Pylos (*c* 1330 B.C.). This would have removed some of the northern leaders to these places, strengthening the central Mycenaean authority there, while these new dynasties would have been under close central control without the concentration of too many ambitious leaders on the northern borders. If such a reconstruction is correct, we have an explanation of the new dynasties from Thessaly without needing to look for hostile action as a cause.

This would also explain why these dynasties were founded far from Thessaly and on the borders of Mycenae when she was at the height of her power. The foundation of a "Phoenician" dynasty at Thebes around 1430 B.C. might have been a recognition of services rendered by the supply of naval power from Phoenicia. It is interesting to note that Herodotus[38] records the tradition that Cadmus came from Tyre.

This policy worked well and guaranteed the northern frontiers until the famous quarrel between Agamemnon and Achilles (*c* 1250) immortalized in the *Iliad,* when the united loyalty of the northern kingdoms was breached, leading to the ultimate disintegration of Mycenaean power.

The end of the Bronze Age marked another important phase in the spread of knowledge and techniques within the Aegean and eastern Mediterranean, for it ushered in the Age of Iron, reviled by Hesiod in bitter terms resembling those often used today of the Atomic Age. The success of the enterprise which culminated in the downfall of Pylos and so many Mycenaean kingdoms called ideally for three conditions: a hardy, warlike people, a strong, intelligent leadership in pursuit of a cause, and superior armaments. The first was provided by the Dorians and their allies, the second by the Heracleidae, and the third may have been the use of iron weapons, probably obtained from t hemilitary stores seized at the collapse of the Hittite empire.

Of course, it can be asked why this should explain the fall of the Mycenaean kingdoms when it could not equally apply to the downfall of the Hittite empire, which after all possessed iron weapons already. The answer is that conditions were very different. The Mycenaean confederation was protected by mountainous approach routes or the sea, making it difficult or impossible to concentrate overwhelming forces against them. The Hittites on the other hand were seriously weakened by decades of warfare on all their borders.

A military hierarchy sometimes remains attached to an outmoded weapon because of misplaced conservatism and the feeling that the new weapon is "not sporting" or "ungentlemanly". Such were the reactions against "filthy gunpowder" and the stand of the cavalryman against the tank. The use of bronze for weapons and armour helped to concentrate power and wealth in the hands of the few as the supply of copper and of tin, essential for the bronze alloy, was limited, needing a well-organized trade to make it available to non-producing areas. This favoured the growth of "divine" kings, together with their hierarchy of feudal nobles and their bureaucracy, which we find described in the Linear B tablets. The capital outlay for bronze weapons and armour would have made it impossible for any uncivilized tribe to equip itself in this way; and no tribe without such armaments would have been able to overrun a nation which possessed bronze and a mobile armed force of chariotry, unless the barbarians had overwhelming superiority of numbers or some other supreme advantage.

Iron was the great leveller, and brought disruption to the organized world of the second millennium B.C. Iron ore is plentiful and widely distributed; once the art of smelting it was known, iron weapons were available to those who could not previously have afforded bronze weapons on a large scale. For smelting iron ore, much higher temperatures are required than for copper, and the injection of a blast of air is needed to reach these. "Meteoric" iron had been known in ancient times, as can be shown by analysis of the earliest artifacts found by archaeologists, but it was extremely rare. The Hittites seem to have been the first to discover the way to smelt iron ore, according to both Mellor and Gurney.[39] The former gives a summary of the history of iron in this period:

> "According to H. Obermaier, the Assyrians obtained their metal from the Caucasus, and the Hittites brought iron into Syria. According to J. de Morgan, the tribes bordering on Armenia and Cappadocia, in the foothills of the Caucasus, discovered the art of smelting iron, where it is possible that a chance admixture of manganese may have yielded a metal of marked excellence. W. Ridgeway said that the Philistines brought iron from these countries into Palestine, and it was there that W. M. F. Petrie, in 1927, discovered the oldest specimens of undoubtedly man-made iron, for in a mound at Gerar, nine miles from Gaza, he found iron-smelting furnaces and agricultural implements, all of which had been made on the spot. These discoveries were dated by means of contemporaneous scarabs and amulets of Egyptian origin; some iron knives are believed to go back to 1350 B.C. and the remains of the furnaces to 1194 B.C."

These dates are very significant, as it would appear that man-made iron existed in this district at the time when the Dorians passed through, and that it was even plentiful enough to be used for making agricultural implements. The apparent date of destruction of the furnaces (*c* 1194 B.C.) coincides with the date we have attributed to the drive towards the Egyptian border, and it is possible to assume that the Dorian invaders would have used such furnaces as arms factories for converting any local scrap iron into weapons, and that the Egyptians would have destroyed them on the repulse of the invaders.

Dealing with the design of furnaces used for metal smelting and working, Mellor[39] goes on to say:

> "According to J. G. Wilkinson, the frescoes of the Egyptian tombs of Beni-Hassan . . . show that prior to the 18th Dynasty the draught in the Egyptian metal furnaces was produced by blow pipes, and four to six men were required for the smelting operations. The mouth blowpieces were made of reeds tipped with clay, and only small pieces of metal could thus be smelted. Bellows were probably introduced about the 18th Dynasty . . . from a tomb (fresco) of the period of Thothmes III, about 1500 B.C. These primitive bellows consisted of a flat pot covered with, presumably, goatskin; there was a hole in the middle of the skin which could be closed by the heel of the operator so as to form a kind of valve; when the valve was released by the heel, the skin was pulled up by a cord in the worker's hand. Similar bellows are used today by some remote tribes in India for the manufacture of iron. The primitive furnaces, or air bloomeries, were erected on high ground in order that the wind might assist combustion."

Gurney quotes[39] a striking passage from a letter sent by the Hittite king Hattusilis III (*c* 1275–1250 B.C.) to a contemporary ruler, believed to have been the king of Assyria:

> "As for the good iron which you wrote about to me, good iron is not available in my seal-house in Kizzuwatna. That it is a bad time for producing iron I have written. They will produce good iron, but as yet they will not have finished. Today now I am dispatching an iron dagger-blade to you."

Gurney ingeniously explains "the bad time for producing iron" by suggesting "that the smelting was carried out by peasants in their homes during the winter season when there was no work to be done in the fields". I believe there is a more technical explanation for such apparently seasonal production. Pending the invention of the forced draught bellows, the Hittites might well have used the high winds, which blow seasonally in the mountains and can be "funnelled" by certain suitable valleys, for the forced draught needed to inject the air. Certainly this technique for smelting copper ore was known about three centuries later in the time of Solomon. Nelson Glueck's excavations[40] at Ezion-geber in the northern part of the Gulf of 'Arabah, have revealed the remains of a copper refinery working on this principle, situated at a point where the north wind down through the 'Arabah was strongest. The furnace brickwork showed that intense heat had been generated and this advanced technique had permitted the use of large clay smelting crucibles with a capacity of fourteen cubic feet. The high value of the metal—in earlier times iron was valued at five to ten times the worth of gold[41]—would have made it worthwhile to allocate labour to its manufacture, while the technique needed skilled specialists rather than rough peasant labour.

The remains of small iron smelters have been found on the mainland of the eastern Mediterranean, but it would seem worthwhile seeking smelters used by the Hittites at suitably windy sites around the Taurus mountains.

After the Hittite empire had been overrun, the knowledge of this process must have gradually spread, and the knowledge of the *working* of iron reached Greece around the Proto-geometric period (from *c* 1075 B.C.), as iron objects begin to be found in graves of that period;[42] previously the metal may have been imported. Several iron rings have been found in Athens with burials of the sub-Mycenaean period, dated around 1125–1075 B.C., and MacKendrick[43] deduces it must still have been a precious metal then. If it is correct that the Dorians brought with them to Pylos iron weapons acquired from the Hittites, there is a gap of about a hundred years to be accounted for between the date of about 1192 B.C. and the time that iron objects were first deposited in graves on the Greek mainland.

It is possible that the Dorians acquired so many iron weapons from the Hittite arsenals that a long time elapsed between their initial conquest of Pylos and the time when their settlement in the Peloponnese was so advanced that they could make them for themselves. It can be assumed that those they brought with them were so superior to bronze that they were too valuable to be buried and therefore grave furniture continued for a long time to include the traditional bronze swords as a ceremonial tribute to the dead. It may be significant that the earliest iron articles from Aegean graves are knives and rings, not functional weapons. If the Dorians brought the Iron Age to Greece they would have husbanded the iron weapons taken from the Hittites for a time before local manufacture began on any scale.

A measure of support for this thesis can be drawn from Snodgrass' recent authoritative survey of early Greek armour and weapons.[44] He makes the point that many of the swords found in Greece show features that can be traced to Cyprus, Crete and the Levant, and that the replacement of bronze by iron swords took place soon after the close of the Bronze Age and "with some abruptness".[45] Referring to the variant of the "Naue II" type of cut-and-thrust sword which tapers evenly from the hilt to the point, and which was almost exclusively Cretan/Cypriot in derivation, he remarks that the style on the mainland was soon changed. Within a relatively short time of the introduction of iron swords of that pattern production was under way of cut-and-thrust iron swords of a similar shape and pattern to the Mycenaean bronze swords which preceded the new weapons. On the other hand there was a gap "of some years" between the latest bronze and earliest iron swords.[44]

The earliest iron swords described comprise: one from Hama in Syria, dated in the period *c* 1200–1075 B.C.; another from Idalion in Cyprus (*c* 1100 B.C.); followed by numerous examples in Attica, Crete and other locations dated to the eleventh and tenth centuries B.C. The Hama sword was the earliest of eleven iron swords (and three bronze ones) found associated with a series of cremations spanning the period *c* 1200–800 B.C., and these swords were of the normal Naue II type with the edges of the blade nearly parallel for the greater part of its length, which was commonly found on the Greek mainland. A remarkable feature is the high proportion of these swords of Naue II type which have been found in Crete, Thessaly and Macedonia.[44] This distribution is consistent with the thesis that the Dorians brought back iron weapons from the expedition of "The Peoples of the Sea" *c* 1192 B.C., that part of the plunder found its way back to the homelands of the Dorians and their allies, and that the contacts opened at that time by the Dorians with Asia Minor were maintained, however sporadically. This chain of contact ran through Crete, Rhodes, Cyprus and the mainland settlements so that subsequent imports of both iron weapons and technical knowledge of their manufacture were gradually built up until ultimately their production could be established in the Greek mainland and the islands en route.

Meantime, the experts in iron smelting and fabrication drawn from the wreckage of the Hittite empire, whom the Dorians would have taken back with them to the mainland, are unlikely to have instituted any large-scale smelting of iron ore in the initial period. Their main energies would undoubtedly have been directed to the servicing of existing weapons, and the refabrication of scrap metal into new swords whose type would have corresponded more with the design of Mycenaean bronze swords with which the mainland Greeks were familiar. During this initial period, pending the local smelting of iron ore on any scale, the iron weapons and scrap metal derived from them would have been too valuable to have been used as grave furnishings. Hence a gap of one hundred years or so is understandable before iron swords became plentiful enough to be used for that purpose.

Religious practices were also involved in this "cross fertilization". The prominent role of Apollo in Dorian affairs is well known and centred on their traditional association with Delphi, one of his most important shrines. Apollo's origin is variously given as the northern regions beyond the Grecian frontiers or as Asia Minor. Professor Gilbert Murray suggested over 35 years ago that a compromise could be found if Apollo was derived from *both* regions. Seltman has pointed out more recent evidence to support this;[46] he mentions that in the early Dorian-Greek dialect Apollo was called "Apellon" and that the Hittites, in the region bordering on Lycia—which was one of Apollo's strongholds in Asia Minor and the origin of his surname "Lykios"—had a god with a similar name: "Apulunas".

I think this attribution of a joint origin for Apollo—both northern and eastern—fits well with the theme (see Chapter 7) that the Minyans came from the north and split into two streams entering northern

Greece originally, and the Troad and southern Greece later. If Apollo came with the Minyans—the first Greek-speaking people to enter the country—then his greater importance for the Dorians, who developed in the northern regions of Greece, is logical; so is the role Homer attributes to him as the patron deity of the Trojans, and so are his Lycian affinities. Bearing all this, and the power of "cross fertilization", in mind, we can reconcile Professor Guthrie's view[47] that the evidence for an Anatolian origin for Apollo seems to be strong, with an ultimate northern origin.

At the fall of the Mycenaean empire about 1192 B.C., the patron deity of the Mycenaeans may have been Poseidon (see Chapter 5), together with the great Nature or Mother Goddess who had eastern affiliations. Palmer[48] has commented on this possible association and found supporting evidence in the Pylian Linear B tablets. But the patron deity of the Dorians was Apollo, and later, during the Greek Renaissance, the Athenians and the Spartans, representatives of the former Mycenaean and Dorian cultures respectively, paid homage to him. Probably with the fall of the Mycenaean empire the cult of Poseidon passed its peak, while Apollo's influence strengthened so that we now find two important shrines to him, each with political associations.

Evidently the Athenians recognized his power and influence, since he brought the Dorians victory. As well as the shrine at Delphi there was one at Delos, in the Mycenaean and Athenian zone. Here, too, we find Artemis associated with him. This also suggests that the Minyan influence came from the north and blended with the culture of the earlier inhabitants who had probably come from Asia Minor to Greece and Crete, bringing with them the "Mother Goddess" and the associated "Boy King". So the Dorians, with a predominantly northern influence, favoured Apollo and Zeus, and the Athenians, with the surviving traditions of the Mycenaeans and Minoans linked with the eastern "Mother Goddess", retained her as Athena and Artemis but linked these with Apollo. Hutchinson[49] remarks that:

> "Evans often seems to suggest that he regards most representations of goddesses on Minoan seals as personifications of the great mother goddess, but a fairer representation of his views is afforded

> by a quotation from a letter he wrote to Nilsson stating 'I have always in mind the possibility that the goddess who appears in so many relations in Minoan schemes and impersonations may cover what was really regarded as separate deities with separate names equivalent to Artemis, Rhea, Athena, Aphrodite, etc. But as a provisional procedure it is convenient . . . to treat the goddess as essentially the same great Nature Goddess under various aspects—celestial with the dove, chthonic with the snake, etc., etc.' We may recall how the Titan Prometheus in Aeschylus's play refers to 'my mother Themis and Earth, one shape with many names' (Prometheus Vinctus, lines 217 and 218)."

By "cross fertilization", we find Apollo worshipped in Ionia, and above all his sister Artemis at Ephesus.

Apart from the migrations in and around the Aegean after the great disturbances of about 1200, there were other movements to more remote areas, amongst them those which led to the foundation of the Etruscan nation. Tradition records that the Tyrseni, who were a Pelasgian non-Greek-speaking people, lived originally in the north-west Aegean and were believed to have come from Thrace.[50] They were associated with Lydia and Lemnos—where an inscription with affinities to Etruscan has been found—and were reputed to have set sail from Lydia in the time of King Atys of that country.[51] The Tursha mentioned as one of "The Peoples of the Sea" by the Egyptians may well have been Tyrsenians (Turs(c)i).[52] They need not necessarily have come from Tuscany at this time to join the attack on Egypt. It was customary for these peoples to retain their name when they migrated, so they may have migrated to Tuscany later to find a more peaceful homeland in the disturbed conditions after 1200.

Certainly, to anyone who has visited the Etruscan Museums at Florence and Rome, there is a striking resemblance between the earliest artifacts there and those of the Mycenaeans and Minoans. This is particularly true of grave furniture from the earliest Etruscan periods (*c* 800 B.C.) in which we find tiny gold replicas of the Minoan labrys, or double axe, and clay models of shrine or temple with a pitched roof. The decoration of the rooftree may be intended as horns of consecration with the tips stylized as doves' heads. Hall has pointed out some curious resemblances between Etruscan art and that of Anatolia,[53] so perhaps a Lydian source for the Etruscan emigration should not be lightly dismissed.

REFERENCES

[1] Hammond, N. G. L., *A History of Greece to 322 B.C.*, 1959, pp. 24 and 36.
[2] Hutchinson, R. W., *Prehistoric Crete*, Pelican Books, 1962, p. 334f.; Hammond, N. G. L., *ibid*, p. 95.
[3] Palmer, L. R., *Mycenaeans and Minoans*, 1961, p. 232f.
[4] Gordon, C. H., *Before the Bible*, 1962, p. 210f.
[5] Gordon, C. H., *op. cit.*
[6] Woolley, L., *A Forgotten Kingdom*, Pelican Books, 1953, p. 75.
[7] MacKendrick, P., *The Greek Stones Speak*, 1962, p. 132f.
[8] Desborough, V. R. d'A., *The Last Mycenaeans and Their Successors*, 1964, p. 229f.
[9] Desborough, V. R. d'A., *ibid*, p. 198f.
[10] Desborough, V. R. d'A., *ibid*, p. 199.
[11] Albright, W. F., *The Archaeology of Palestine*, Pelican Books, 1960, p. 185.
[12] Albright, W. F., *ibid*, p. 115; Desborough, V. R. d'A., *ibid*, pp. 209f, 214 and 240.
[13] Woolley, L., *ibid*, p. 61.
[14] Gordon, C. H., *ibid*, p. 24.
[15] Hutchinson, R. W., *ibid*, p. 164f.
[16] Hutchinson, R. W., *ibid*, p. 193.
[17] Gurney, O. R., *The Hittites*, Pelican Books, 1961, p. 19f.
[18] Hutchinson, R. W., *ibid*, p. 173.
[19] Hutchinson, R. W., *ibid*, pp. 187 and 193.
[20] Woolley, L., *ibid*, p. 74f.
[21] Hutchinson, R. W., *ibid*, p. 178f.
[22] Daily Telegraph, 24 September 1963.
[23] Gurney, O. R., *ibid*, p. 23.
[24] Mylonas, G. E., *Ancient Mycenae*, 1957, p. 181.
[25] Mylonas, G. E., *ibid*, p. 175.
[26] Hall, H. R., *The Ancient History of the Near East*, 1960, p. 56.
[27] Hutchinson, R. W., *ibid*, p. 282.
[28] Gurney, O. R., *ibid*, p. 29.
[29] Gurney, O. R., *ibid*, p. 30.
[30] Mylonas, G. E., *ibid*, p. 66.
[31] MacKendrick, P., *ibid*, p. 76.
[32] Desborough, V. R. d'A., *ibid*, pp. 158f and 205f.
[33] Woolley, L., *ibid*, p. 171f.

[34] Thucydides, *The Peloponnesian War,* Bantam Classics, 1960, Book I, p. 26.
[35] Hammond, N. G. L., *ibid,* p. 60.
[36] Herodotus, *The Histories,* The Penguin Classics, 1963, Book VI, p. 378.
[37] Desborough, V. R. d'A., *ibid,* p. 128.
[38] Herodotus, *ibid,* Book II, p. 122.
[39] Mellor, J. W., *A Comprehensive Treatise on Inorganic and Theoretical Chemistry,* Volume XII, p. 491; and Gurney, O. R, *ibid,* p. 83.
[40] Albright, W. F., *ibid,* p. 127f.
[41] Seton Lloyd, *Early Anatolia,* Pelican Books, 1956, pp. 99 and 118.
[42] Desborough, V. R. d'A., *ibid,* p. 70.
[43] MacKendrick, P., *ibid,* p. 127.
[44] Snodgrass, A., *Early Greek Armour and Weapons,* 1964, pp. 108 and 191.
[45] Snodgrass, A., *ibid,* p. 103.
[46] Seltman, C., *The Twelve Olympians,* Pan Books, 1961, p. 110f.
[47] Palmer, L. R., *ibid,* p. 245f.
[48] Palmer, L. R., *ibid,* p. 127f.
[49] Hutchinson, R. W., *ibid,* p. 207.
[50] Hall, H. R., *ibid,* p. 336; Hammond, N. G. L., *ibid,* p. 57.
[51] Herodotus, *ibid,* Book I, p. 53.
[52] Hall, H. R., *ibid,* p. 70.
[53] Hall, H. R., *ibid,* p. 336.

CHAPTER TEN

A Short Chronological History of the Rise and Fall of the Mycenaean Empire

As the generation of leaves, so is that of men

HOMER

IN order to clarify the pattern of events we have considered, it will be useful to summarize all the dates in a chronological tabulation so that the sequence of events can be better appreciated. Three dates have been taken as key points: the great eruption of the island of Thera as *c* 1450 B.C., the fall of Troy as *c* 1250 B.C., and the invasion of Egypt by "The Peoples of the Sea" and the initial stage of the Dorian invasions—leading to the destruction of Pylos—as *c* 1192 B.C. The reasons for taking these dates, and the aid of the authorities invoked, have already been cited (Chapters 3, 4 and 5). These dates are not immutable, and subsequent researches may well modify them.

In particular, the date of *c* 1192 B.C. for the invasion of Egypt does not imply that this is fixed accurately to the year. It is simply the date customarily assigned to this event, with a reasonable degree of accuracy, as Egyptian dates for this period are well-established by their astronomical records. In assigning the date of *c* 1192 B.C. to the destruction of Pylos I am not presuming to correct Blegen's authoritative date of *c* 1200 B.C., which is, of course, a "rounded-off" figure. The more specific date is taken because it fits with the course of other events elsewhere as developed in the theory (Chapter 3), while *c* 1192 B.C. and *c* 1200 B.C. must be considered as being "the same dates" within the recognized error of measurement. In fact the error of measurement can be generally accepted as being of the order of a spread of fifty years under the most favourable circumstances, and in many cases considerably greater. In the summary below I have not repeated the references on which the dates are established, nor the line of reasoning from which they are taken, as these will be found in the previous text dealing with the events in question.

c 2500–c 1900 B.C. The incursion of the first Greeks—the Minyans—into the Greek mainland, the Cyclades and the Troad (Chapter 7).

c 1800–c 1450 B.C. Rise and fall of the Minoan empire. Period during which the Minoan Thalassocracy came into being and Minoan cultural, and possibly political, influence extended to the mainland (Chapter 9).

c 1600 B.C. Start of the rise of the Mycenaean power on the Greek mainland. Possible influence of the royal house of Epaphus (*c* 1520 B.C.) (Chapter 9).

c 1450 B.C. Destruction of the Minoan fleet and disruption of main centres of government in Crete as a result of the great eruption in the island of Thera, followed by seizure of the stricken Minoan empire by Mycenaeans (Chapter 5). Possible recompense of Mycenaean allies by the award of the kingdoms of Orchomenos and Thebes arising from Mycenaean expansion northwards. It is also possible that Dorian allies of the Mycenaeans in the Cretan invasion were allocated lands in eastern Crete and that a branch of the Heracleidae was awarded the Minoan settlements in Rhodes and associated areas (Chapter 9).

c 1430–1330 B.C. Consolidation of Mycenaean power in the northern kingdoms and strengthening of Mycenaean empire by dynastic awards of Peloponnesian kingdoms (Corinth and Pylos) to supporters from Thessaly (Chapter 9).

c 1320 B.C. The "Dorians" under King Deukalion recorded as living at this period in southern Thessaly and the region of Phthiotis (Chapter 8).

c 1300 B.C. The kingdom of Troy weakened by a violent earthquake which destroyed the city (Troy VI) (Chapter 7). Around 1300 B.C. (Tawagalawas letter) Hittite relations with Achaeans were friendly and the influence of the king of Mycenae extended to Asia Minor. Possibly Troy was affiliated with the Mycenaean empire (Chapter 2).

c 1280 B.C. Internal struggle for power within the Mycenaean kingdoms leads to the fall of Thebes and the rise of Mycenae to the control of the Mycenaean confederation, setting the stage for the "Wars of the Roses". Noble Theban families and the Heracleidae flee northwards and become leaders of the Dorians. Thebes subordinated to Mycenae (Chapter 6).

c 1280 B.C. Expanding Mycenaean power in Iolkos, Orchomenos and Thebes expels the Dorians from the region of Phthiotis and drives them northwards to the regions surrounding Ossa and Olympus known as Histiaeotis (Chapter 8). Archaeological evidence from Thessaly and Macedonia indicates that the Dorians were Mycenaeans, or at least "fringe" Mycenaeans, with the ruling element having stronger affinities in this direction than their "north-west" Greek henchmen.

c 1260 B.C. Abortive attempt by the Dorians under the leadership of Hyllus on the Isthmus of Corinth, apparently taking advantage of the Mycenaean forces' absence in the Troad. Start of the "Wars of the Roses" or Trojan War in which Dorians were Trojan allies or at least sympathizers (Chapters 5, 6 and 8). Rhodes, under one branch of the Heracleidae, sides with the Mycenaeans.

c 1250 B.C. Dorians driven out of the region of Ossa and Olympus and displaced northwards and westwards into Macedonia and the Pindus region, which they may already have controlled. This displacement may have been a reprisal for the raid of Hyllus and the attitude of the Dorians in the Trojan War (Chapter 8).

c 1250 B.C. Defeat of the Trojan allies by the Mycenaean confederation under King Agamemnon and capture of the city of Troy (Settlement VIIa) (Chapter 7).

c 1250–1220 B.C. Relations between the king of Mycenae (Achaeans) and the Hittites become first strained and then hostile (Chapter 2).

c 1250–1220 B.C. The Mycenaean confederation was progressively weakened during this period by internal rivalries and dissensions, aggravated by overexpansion into Asia Minor at the expense of the ruins of the Trojan alliance and of the Hittite sphere of influence on the Mediterranean seaboard (Chapter 7).

c 1221 B.C. Mycenaean influence extends to Cyprus which experiences a period of prosperity. Participation by Achaeans (Mycenaeans) in the abortive attack on Egypt by "The Peoples of the Sea" in alliance with the Libyans, using Cyprus as an advanced base. Repulse of this attack further weakens Mycenaean power, particularly in Asia Minor (Chapter 7).

c 1220 B.C. The "Myrmidons" under the noble clan of Achilles break away from the Mycenaean confederation as an ultimate consequence or the "Wrath of Achilles". Probably Rhodes also secedes about this time, as a result of the Egyptian fiasco, and links up with kinsmen—the Heracleidae—leading the Dorians. Probably around this time the Dorians press southwards and reoccupy the areas around Olympus and Ossa.

c 1195 B.C. Dorians and their allies erupt into Asia Minor, and are welcomed as liberators by Trojans and their allies from the Trojan War. Collapse of Hittite empire, weakened by continuous wars on all fronts with Egyptians, Mycenaeans and the wild Kaskan tribesmen on their northern borders (Chapters 2 and 7).

c 1195–1192 B.C. The Dorians and their allies, reinforced by the peoples and weapons of the kingdoms overrun, press southwards, ultimately mounting an attack on Egypt. Apart from Rhodes several of the Mycenaean settlements bordering the north-eastern coastline of the Mediterranean join the movement (no destruction). However, Myceneaean Cyprus is attacked by Dorians, but occupation only temporary.

c 1195–1100 B.C. New kingdoms formed in Asia Minor, Syria and Palestine on the ruins of the old. The Phrygians (or Muski) become heirs to the Hittite homeland, the Hittites are displaced southwards and form the neo-Hittite kingdoms in their old dependencies in Syria and its borders, and the Philistines and Phoenicians inherit the coastal regions further south.

c 1192 B.C. Repulse of the Dorians and their allies ("The Peoples of the Sea") by Ramesses III on the Egyptian border.

c 1192 B.C. The Dorians and their allies, under leadership of the Heracleidae, reinforced by arms and men from the wreckage of the kingdoms of Asia Minor and Syria, take the sea-route homewards. Thus the thrust towards Egypt is converted into a raid in force on Pylos and possibly on Crete first, during the return home.

c 1192 B.C. Success of this raid on Pylos converts it into an occupation —the "return of the Heracleidae". Possible sack of Knossos and other Cretan towns, en route to Pylos, but no occupation of the island by Dorians yet (Chapters 4 and 5).

c 1192–1180 B.C. Dorian invaders in the Peloponnese make contact with their homeland in the Pindus area initially via the Gulf of Ambracia, establishing themselves round the Gulf and to the south and in the offshore islands. Communications with the Dorian homeland also opened up through the "traditional" route via the Gulf of Corinth,

Delphi, Boeotia and Iolkos. Together with reinforcements of their kinsmen and their allies, the "north-west" Greeks (coming respectively via Corinthia and the west coast of the peninsula), they extend and consolidate their hold on the Peloponnese peninsula. Athens holds out. Dorians concentrate in Peloponnese leaving Thessaly and Boeotia to be occupied by their northern Greek allies (Chapter 8).

c 1190 B.C. Commencement of the Aeolic migrations, comprising those Mycenaean elements who found *Anschluss* with the Dorians unwelcome, or who wished to take over areas in "Aeolis" in Asia Minor which were masterless as a result of the passage of "The Peoples of the Sea" (Chapter 8).

c 1180–1150 B.C. Mycenaean culture in Peloponnese continues without interruption, demonstrating the Mycenaean affinities of the ruling element amongst the Dorians. Severe depopulation of this area, largely attributable to an outbreak of plague as well as famine, as a consequence of the invasion. Shifts of population occur away from the stricken areas and the zones most vulnerable to sea-raids by the opposing sides, so concentration of population occurs in "safe" areas centred on the internal communications and respective zones of influence. Thus the Dorians tended to concentrate in Achaea and Kephallenia, and the Mycenaeans in eastern Attica (Perati) and the Aegean islands under their control (Chapter 4).

c 1160–1150 B.C. The Dorians, having consolidated their position in the Peloponnese, extend their influence to the Mycenaean islands of Cythera and Thera, subsequently including those roughly south of a line drawn from Melos to Halicarnassus. Probably Rhodes had been mastered by the Dorians (Heracleidae) in earlier times before the Trojan War, and Casos and Carpathos were possibly retained *c* 1192 B.C. if not before. They occupy the richest parts of Crete, driving the inhabitants into the wilder parts where "Cities of Refuge" are set up. Later the Dorian occupation is extended to the coasts of Asia Minor centring on Cnidus and Halicarnassus (Chapters 5 and 8).

c 1150 or 1130–c 1125 B.C. The "northern" element of the Dorians increasingly gains control over the Heracleidian nations, culminating in the final "Granary" destruction of Mycenae (*c* 1150 or 1130 B.C.), and the flight of their Mycenaean masters, together with some of the remaining Mycenaean elements in the areas occupied by the Dorians, to the remaining Mycenaean centres of Attica (such as the Kerameikos quarter at Athens) and Cyprus (Chapter 4).

c 1070 B.C. Commencement of the Ionic migrations as a consequence of the immigration of Mycenaean refugees into Athens and subsequent expansion of population (Chapter 8).

c 1050 B.C. First major invasion from the north down the valley of the river Axios, representing the first disturbance of Dorian control of the northern areas (Chapter 4).

c 1050–c 900 B.C. "Cities of Refuge" in Crete peacefully abandoned as the Dorian conquerors merge with the previous inhabitants (Chapter 5).

The archaeological record relating to these events is dealt with in connection with their discussion above. However, it is useful at this point to summarize some of the main features. Many variations of the main theme are possible. For instance, the Dorians, under the leadership of the Heracleidae, might have attacked Pylos and the other Mycenaean kingdoms after the Hittite empire and Asia Minor had been overrun, but *before* the invasion of Egypt *c* 1192 B.C. In that case, the date for the fall of Pylos would have to be updated by a few years, perhaps to *c* 1195 B.C.

However, I think this unlikely for a number of reasons. One gathers from the wording of the contemporary Egyptian record that the fall of the Hittite empire and the advance to the Egyptian border took place as one continuous chain of events. Indeed, once the southward movement had gathered momentum it is logical to assume that it would have carried through until it spent itself against the Egyptian counter-attack. Moreover, if the assault on Egypt had indeed followed rather than preceded the invasion of Pylos, it would have involved launching a further large naval movement. I think it extremely improbable that this could have been done after the fall of Pylos, as the Dorians would have been fully occupied attacking the remaining Mycenaean kingdoms. It would also have involved leaving their new conquests undefended with Athens still not subdued but hostile. Taking into account also the psychological urge to settle down and enjoy their hard-won gains in the Peloponnese, I do not think that the Dorians would have done this.

CHAPTER ELEVEN

The Birth Pangs of Democracy

Power tends to corrupt and absolute power corrupts absolutely

BARON ACTON

THE growth of civilization in the areas bordering the eastern Mediterranean can be divided, after its initial stages, into three phases:

1. The period of the Temple Kings.
2. The period of Kings under Divine Protection.
3. The period of the City States.

With the close of each stage a further step was taken towards democracy as we know it today. When man first began to settle on the land, and to raise crops and herds on it, the seed of urban growth was planted. These first steps in organized agriculture called for an increasing number of specialists, to manufacture the tools and amenities of life required, and for a strong and intelligent central control to organize the division of labour between the fields and workshops, as well as the trade which grew out of them, and the defence which was soon needed to preserve the growing wealth of the community from the envy of competitors or less civilized peoples.

This initial step led to the creation of the states of the "Temple Kings" in which the control of the state was centred round a figure who wielded absolute power and claimed divine right for it. He was either a "Priest King" with the organization built round the Temple, or a king credited with being divine and ruling in close conjunction with the Temples. This was apparently a natural growth from the days of prehistoric man as, with the organization of hunting and then of agriculture, the human race demanded some spiritual explanation of the manifestations of nature. The passage of the seasons, their success or failure, was of the greatest importance to man's material comfort. Their cycle, each with its influence, good or bad, on the results of hunting and agriculture, called for an explanation.

Prehistoric man found this first in "sympathetic magic" and then in the explanation of supernatural influence. The former led to the tribal medicine man and cave paintings; and the medicine man evolved ultimately into the "Priest King" whose control of the community progressed from organizing the tribal magical ceremonies to being the supreme representative of the national deities. As such he was charged with the task of organizing the Temple and its concomitant functions of regulating the seasonal processes of agriculture, often together with the specialized arts and techniques called for by an organized community.

This central control led to the development of cities where the Temple was the focus of activity, with associated workshops where the specialists could devote all their energies to their particular activity while still receiving their share of rations provided from the agricultural and hunting pursuits of the rest of the community. This marked a big step forward in the development of civilization, as in addition to its material benefits it also satisfied a spiritual need, since all efforts were directed towards and controlled by the Temple under divine authority. Yet it was just this which flawed an otherwise promising evolution, as the human tendency to overdo matters ultimately led to absolute power being concentrated in the central authority with too great a proportion of the wealth created syphoned off to provide the attributes of worship. Thus custom and tradition froze into divine laws, and inventiveness and initiative were stifled by the Temple establishment so that progress came to a halt. The ancient Egyptian civilization is an outstanding example of this.

Human progress seems to be governed by a relationship similar to that of Planck's law in the realm of physics—the progress of a system is not one of continuous regular development forward but results from the release of periodic bursts of energy. The next big advance in civilization seems to have come through the modification of the "Temple Kings" system to one where we find a secular king with divine overtones and attributes. This is depicted in the Linear B tablets, a situation which, I believe, we must attribute to a fusion between the Indo-European tribal structure and the Temple organization of the Near East. This fusion arose at their points of contact in Asia Minor and Syria (see Chapter 9) and was due to the Minyans and their descendants, particularly as far as Greece is concerned. At first sight the transition may not seem important: from a Priest-King to a King-Priest. But it gave scope for a broadening of the central authority with emphasis no longer entirely on the religious aspects.

The world of the Linear B tablets, as strikingly interpreted by Palmer, resembles an Indo-European tribal structure[1] (which ultimately evolved into the feudal system of the Middle Ages), where we find a noble hierarchy of barons with a war leader, owing allegiance to the king, and owning land in return for military service. In addition we have the *damos*—the common man—owning land collectively, and finally Temple lands as a separate entity. Not for nothing does Homer make Nausicaa tell Odysseus, when he is cast away on the shores of the land of the Phaeacians, that the layout of the city of her father King Alcinous includes a separate temple to Poseidon with the peoples' meeting place on either side of it, and with a separate palace for her father. However, as Palmer[2] points out, in Nausicaa's description, land owned by King Alcinous—his *temenos*—is linked with the adjoining poplar grove sacred to Athena. Palmer[3] also makes the important point that the tablets show that the *damos* was not completely subservient to the religious organization, as a pair of texts record a dispute between the priestess and the *damos* over whether a piece of land is owned by the god or alternatively owned by the *damos* and leased to the priestess. It is vital to the point we are considering here that the priestess is speaking for the god and that apparently the protest is recorded in the palace records of the king, here acting in his secular function.

In the cross fertilization discussed in Chapter 9 the Greeks (or Minyans) had taken over many of the constructive features of the Temple organization, such as the bureaucracy of land and cattle ownership, of distribution of rations and of records of stores, equipment and weapons, together with the running of the workshops producing them. All this was recorded in tablets held in the royal archives whose discovery at Knossos, Pylos and elsewhere has given us so much information as vividly described by Palmer and others.[4] I think that it was this happy marriage of the freer tribal organization of the Minyans with the rigidly-organized Temple system which gave the first important step towards a democratic state. On the one hand there was the Indo-European, recognizing a social organization of king and barons but insisting that the *damos* should participate in affairs, however slightly. On the other we have the Temple with its records and organization, but frozen into a rigid pattern directed to one end. The fusion of these two gave a stronger and more progressive society.

It has been pointed out[5] that the picture of the *damos* we obtain from the Linear B tablets is not supported by the incident in the *Iliad* when Odysseus beats Thersites for daring to suggest in the Assembly that the Greeks abandon the siege of Troy. But Palmer points out that in the field the commoner was ill-advised to run counter to the princely warriors. Indeed, this incident can be seen better if we think what would have happened in World War I under our own democratic system. The man would probably have been shot.

Under Mycenaean rule this new system naturally led to a greater sharing of the wealth of the community. For this reason I think that the relative strength and organization of the Mycenaean states were greater than would appear at first sight from their archaeological relics compared with those of the Temple states. It is possible that the Minoan system of government was already less rigid in structure, but the system was still further modified under Mycenaean control where the Indo-European tribal structure introduced a new and vital element. After the Mycenaeans seized power in Crete *c* 1450 B.C. the concentration of the communities' wealth in the palaces diminished or lapsed entirely, but this does not mean that the wealth and activity of the island as a whole was adversely affected. In this respect Palmer[6] is probably correct in thinking that in the LM III period, after the Mycenaean conquest, Crete was no backwater but a flourishing Achaean power, as witnessed by the proven export of inscribed jars to the mainland, and of bronze ware to Pylos, as recorded in the tablets. It is no accident that the archaeological evidence from Gournia, in the east of the island, shows that a flourishing industrial town, by the standards of that period, grew up round the nucleus of the Palace, after the LM Ia period[7] (i.e. after *c* 1500 B.C.), which had itself meantime been "democratized". As MacKendrick[8] put it:

> "This petty king kept his vassals at no greater distance than would a medieval lord."

With the greater Mycenaean emphasis on individual responsibility, we find in the Linear B tablets a pyramidical structure of feudal barons under the king, served by retainers; a structure which offered more scope for individual development. This lent itself to the formation of a confederation of kingdoms owing allegiance to a High King (the classic example being Agamemnon), another example of the Indo-European tribal structure. It is reminiscent of the early Middle Ages in France, when the dukes and barons—who were in effect petty kings—owed an allegiance to the "High King" in Paris which was strong or weak in proportion to the king's strength of character and resources. The Mycenaean system contrasted favourably with the Temple states where the tendency was to conquer neighbouring states, or to rule them through an imposed vassal king.

The Mycenaean system worked well, and as Desborough[9] has pointed out, undoubtedly led to a powerful empire which controlled from Mycenae the whole Aegean area and was able to operate in Asia Minor. This empire was able to conquer Crete and its possessions (*c* 1450 B.C.), destroy Troy and its allies (*c* 1250 B.C.) and apparently participate with the Libyans in a raid in force on Egypt (*c* 1221 B.C.). All this called for a considerable degree of manpower organization and planning logistics which should not be underestimated. The first two events led to an expansion of empire, which included increased influence on the Greek mainland towards the north. Events leading up to the second phase resulted in the subjugation of Thebes, and the ejection of the "Dorians" from the area of Phthiotis northwards and ultimately also westwards, so that at least the southern coastal areas of Thessaly were incorporated in the empire and its influence extended beyond. Thus the period *c* 1450–1250 B.C. saw the Mycenaean empire reach its height by the time of the Trojan War and include all the countries in Homer's Catalogue of the Achaean allies in the *Iliad*. It is even possible (see Chapter 7) that for a short time after the fall of Troy the empire included Troy itself, and the lands of some of the Trojan allies, until the whole structure collapsed from internal dissensions and the culmination of the Dorian feud.

Such a flexible federation still suffered from the disadvantage that too much wealth and power were concentrated in the hands of the ruling kings and their noble barons supported by their feudal followers. The seeds of decay lay within the system itself. The *degree* of concentration of wealth with the ruling hierarchy became too great as the state prospered and wealth grew. The structure was vulnerable at one point—the whole system depended on the strength and wisdom of the High King and the lack of a powerful enough rival within the confederation to challenge his supremacy. I believe it was recognition of this that led Homer to take the "Wrath of Achilles" as the central theme of the *Iliad* because of the fatal consequences of the greed and pride of Agamemnon which caused the breach with Achilles. As discussed in Chapter 6, I think it was this lack of statesmanship shown by Agamemnon—the "High King" of the Mycenaean confederation—which caused a realignment of the balance of forces in the Mycenaean world, and led the clan of Achilles to defect and make common cause with the Heracleidae. This weakening of the northern marches of the empire started the final phase in the Greek "Wars of the Roses" and initiated the chain of events (Chapters 3 and 8) which led to the march of "The Peoples of the Sea", the fall of Pylos and the ultimate Dorian invasions.

Strangely enough, the next step forward—the rise of the City State—must be attributed to the chaos which followed the disintegration of the Mycenaean empire. The serious depopulation, particularly of the Argolid and the Peloponnese and its dependencies generally, the result of war, plague and famine, must have resembled that in England after the Black Death. The serf in the country could put a higher value on his services and place in the community, supported by the hardihood bred from so much death and suffering. The impact would have been greater still in the Mycenaean empire. Defeats and disasters would have seriously weakened popular belief in the divine support of the rulers. The subsequent infiltration of the less civilized northern element of the Dorians, whose Indo-European tribal organization had a lesser infusion of Mycenaean culture than the original invaders led by the Heracleidae, would have strengthened the tendency for a secular rather than a divine kingship. Thus of the three supports for the Mycenaean system, the king under divine protection, the noble barons, and the *damos,* the first two crumbled before the disasters following the Dorian invasions and the last benefited correspondingly.

Even in the last stronghold of the Mycenaeans, the kingdom of Athens itself, which apparently held out against the invaders, we learn from Greek tradition that the line of Attic kings ended with Codrus, who successfully defended the city from the Dorians. It is evident that the consequences of the Dorian disasters were so widespread and profound that they spread throughout the whole Greek world and affected friend and foe alike. Of course the Greek City State did not flourish unopposed, and from time to time kings or tyrants seized power and endured for a while. However the germ of the idea began to grow and in the suffering and chaos of the Dark Ages the first principles of democracy were formed. These, with their new freedom for the individual, led to the evolution of the philosopher and to the use of the written word for the expression of ideas rather than mainly for the recording of stores and religious rituals. From this combination we can trace the rise of civilization as we know it, and we can reflect with some irony that it was the pain and suffering of the Dark Ages which spurred mankind to take this step forward. It was in fact the Dorians who unwittingly began the movement.

REFERENCES

[1] Palmer, L. R., *Mycenaeans and Minoans,* 1961, p. 90f.

[2] *Ibid,* p. 95.

[3] *Ibid,* p. 97.

[4] *Op. cit.*

[5] *Ibid,* p. 98.

[6] *Ibid,* p. 225.

[7] Hutchinson, R. W., *Prehistoric Crete,* Pelican Books, 1962, p. 289.

[8] MacKendrick, P., *The Greek Stones Speak,* 1962, p. 104.

[9] Desborough, V. R. d'A., *The Last Mycenaeans and Their Successors,* 1964, p. 218f.

Index

A

Place-names shown in *italics* will be found on the two endpaper maps by means of the grid-references given there.

B

C

Place-names shown in *italics* will be found on the two endpaper maps by means of the grid-references given there.

D

Place-names shown in *italics* will be found on the two endpaper maps by means of the grid-references given there.

E

F

Place-names shown in *italics* will be found on the two endpaper maps by means of the grid-references given there.

G

H

Place-names shown in *italics* will be found on the two endpaper maps by means of the grid-references given there.

I

K

Place-names shown in *italics* will be found on the two endpaper maps by means of the grid-references given there.

Place-names shown in *italics* will be found on the two endpaper maps by means of the grid-references given there.

N

O

P

Place-names shown in *italics* will be found on the two endpaper maps by means of the grid-references given there.

Place-names shown in *italics* will be found on the two endpaper maps by means of the grid-references given there.

R

S

Place-names shown in *italics* will be found on the two endpaper maps by means of the grid-references given there.

V

W

X

Y

Z

Place-names shown in *italics* will be found on the two endpaper maps by means of the grid-references given there.

OCT 2 2 1978
DISCHARGED
DISCHARGED
DISCHARGED
FEB 2 4 1975
DISCHARGED
MAR 3 1975
MAR 1 0 1975
DISCHARGED
DISCHARGED
DISCHARGED
DISCHARGED
APR 2 6 1976